Canada's Catholics

Vitality and Hope in a New Era

Reginald W. Bibby and Angus Reid

NOVALIS

Cover design and layout: Audrey Wells
Cover photograph: W.P. Wittman
Interior images: Courtesy of the individual or organization featured. Used with permission.

Published by Novalis

Publishing Office
10 Lower Spadina Avenue, Suite 400
Toronto, Ontario, Canada
M5V 2Z2

Head Office
4475 Frontenac Street
Montréal, Québec, Canada
H2H 2S2

www.novalis.ca

Library and Archives Canada Cataloguing in Publication

Reid, Angus, author
Canada's Catholics : vitality and hope in a new era / Angus Reid and Reginald Bibby.

Includes bibliographical references and index.
ISBN 978-2-89688-261-8 (paperback)

1. Catholic Church--Canada--History. 2. Catholics--Religious identity--Canada--History. 3. Church renewal--Catholic Church. I. Bibby, Reginald W. (Reginald Wayne), author II. Title.

BX1421.3.R43 2016 282'.71 C2015-908420-2

Printed in Canada.

We acknowledge the financial support of the Government of Canada through the Canada Book Fund for business development activities.

5 4 3 2 1 20 19 18 17 16

Table of Contents

Foreword

A wise old saying that I have always found immensely valuable is "If you know where you are going, you are more likely to get there." When it comes to Christian discipleship, and to leadership of the Church, we discover where we need to go through prayer and through deep reflection on the Word of God encountered in the Bible and in the living tradition of the Church, in the doctrines of the faith that guide us, and in the lives of the saints who inspire us. The encounter with Christ transforms our lives, although the Christian path in life will always be countercultural, and people may well walk away when they are confronted with its challenges, as they did when Jesus was among us in Galilee. We cannot adjust the faith to attract them. If, however, they walk away because our own failings as individuals or as a faith community block the light of Christ, then we need to learn from that and see how we can remedy the situation.

This means that essential as it is to discover in Word and Sacrament the stars we steer by, in order that we may know where we are meant to go in God's plan, we also need to have accurate knowledge of where we are right now.

On a personal level, this is not the least of the benefits of a daily examination of conscience, regular daily times of prayer, and frequent confession. But as a Church as well, we need humbly to learn where we are and to shed all illusion and complacency, so that we may get from where we are to where we need to be.

I have always found Reginald Bibby's work most instructive as I seek to understand more truly the current situation of Catholic Christian life in Canada, so that I may be more effective in my ministry as a bishop. Just as grace builds on nature, so evangelization needs to build on accurate information. That is why I have asked Reginald Bibby to speak to the priests of my diocese, so that we might benefit not only from his insights into those who are practising the faith, with whom we are familiar, but even more so from his insights into those who are not. As the fundamental statement of the pastoral plan of the Archdiocese of Toronto puts it: "Care for the gathered, and reach out to the scattered." We can learn a lot about both the gathered and the scattered from Reginald Bibby and his research, as well as from that of Angus Reid.

I have read with great interest *Canada's Catholics*, in which Reginald Bibby and Angus Reid combine their formidable expertise to provide a most useful analysis of the current state of Catholic Christianity in Canada. There is a lot to reflect on in this book, and much immensely valuable information and insight to illuminate both the challenges we face in the mission of evangelization and the opportunities that are offered to us.

It is a fundamental teaching of Catholicism that faith and reason are meant to work together. God has put our heads in so prominent a place on our bodies that he surely wants us to use them. All Catholics can benefit from this perceptive analysis offered by Reginald Bibby and Angus Reid. We may or may not like what we see in the data presented, or agree or disagree with the analysis of particular points, but we will all benefit from a serious engagement with this book.

Thomas Cardinal Collins
Archbishop of Toronto

Preface

One of the fascinating things about life is how seemingly isolated, disparate pieces come together to form something good and unexpected.

In this book, that has happened. We have been plying our respective trades in sociology and survey research for many years without actually meeting each other. We also have travelled different highways in the course of valuing faith and sharing our research with others for whom faith is important.

But, in the proverbial fullness of time, in late 2013 we were brought together by a mutual friend and colleague, Andrew Grenville, and since then have had the opportunity to put our minds and efforts together. This book is one result. But it also reflects some other pieces that have come together … a valued friendship with Cardinal Collins that, for Reg, dates back to his days in Edmonton and study days together with the then Archbishops' priests in Jasper … work with Anne Louise Mahoney on some of the embryonic ideas in this book that appeared in Novalis' *Restless Churches* more than ten years ago … right back to those early days and early grades when Angus and Reg were attending churches with their parents and brothers and sisters in western Canada.

This book represents something of an unanticipated synthesis of it all.

We want to express our appreciation to a number of people who have played a direct role in contributing to the research upon which this book is based, led by Andrew Grenville and Mag Burns. We have greatly appreciated the encouragement and initiative of Joseph Sinasac, the Publishing Director at Novalis, who has quarterbacked the project. We also are so very grateful to Anne Louise Mahoney, our managing editor, who has brought her skills and her always uplifting spirit to the task of moving the manuscript to publication. On a more personal level, we are grateful to our respective wives, Lita and Margaret, for their ongoing support of this project and our lives more generally.

Our hope is that this book will contribute both to a clearer understanding of Catholics in Canada and to an enhancement of ministry and life.

Reginald Bibby & Angus Reid
January 2016

Dedication

To our late parents

Lorna and Ernest Reid

&

Bud and Roberta Bibby

Whose unshakeable faith touched us both deeply,
and echoes across the generations.

Introduction

Many decades ago, as an undergraduate student, I was faced with a career decision that would turn out to have a tremendous impact on the direction of my life in the ensuing half-century. The choice was between economics and sociology: understanding financial flows and economic systems versus human values and social structures. The one event that helped tip the scales to the latter career was a study I came across in the late 1960s by Charles Glock and Rodney Stark, entitled *Christian Beliefs and Anti-Semitism*. Here was the science of polling shining a light on an issue that had been debated since the Second World War: to what extent were Christian beliefs (Christ was killed by the Jews) implicated in the anti-Semitism that provided fertile ground for the Holocaust?

I grew up in a devout Catholic family of eight kids. As a student at a Jesuit college, I was immersed in the changes under way in what would become known as Vatican II – the end of Latin masses and meatless Fridays, and the start of a new movement that placed some of the more controversial moral issues of that era, such as birth control, squarely in the conscience of individuals. For me, Vatican II was all about including the Catholic laity in the rituals and morality of our Church.

After a brief stint as a university professor, I formed a survey research company that in various incarnations has been monitoring the pulse of Canadians on a wide variety of issues for the better part of 50 years. Through this time, I have never abandoned my interest in the subject of religious beliefs. In the 1980s, my colleague Andrew Grenville and I conducted a major study on Christian beliefs and political choice across North America to learn whether Orthodox and Evangelical Christians were more likely to support parties on the right of the political spectrum ("yes" in the United States; "no" in Canada). In 1993, we collaborated with *Maclean's* magazine on a cover story on religious beliefs and experience in Canada. At the time, the "God is Alive" issue produced reader mail that ranked this issue in the top 10 in the magazine's history.

During the early stages of my career, I kept hearing the name of another sociologist, operating out of the University of Lethbridge in southern Alberta, who was producing a large body of research and literature on the same topic. Through the years, Reg Bibby has become the leading expert on the religious beliefs and practices of Canadians. His work is widely cited in academic circles, in newsrooms and among church leaders who have drawn on his insights to help define strategy and ministry.

In late 2014, with my new research foundation – the Angus Reid Institute – in its infancy, we decided that one of our early projects would be a major investigation of religion in Canadian society. Some two decades after the *Maclean's* study, we wanted to take stock of what had changed and what the future held for religion in Canada. As we assembled a team of experts for the project, my first call was to Reg, who became an enthusiastic leader and part sponsor of this initiative. The original plan was to carry out interviews with a representative sample of 1,500 Canadians.

Partway through our data collection, Reg came up with an idea that would help to make this book possible – to extend the overall sample to include approximately 1,000 Catholics. This allowed us to generate largely unprecedented data on the beliefs, attitudes and practices of Catholics across the country, including – of course – Quebec. Comprehensive national survey data on Catholics has been sparse, which is somewhat surprising given the historical place of the Church in Canada, especially during the country's formative years.

Media reports in recent decades, for example, have offered at best a confusing picture of the status of Catholicism in Canada. Scandals involving sexual abuse continued to receive widespread coverage in the early part of the new millennium, while debates over women's roles and priestly celibacy took on new energy in the face of what was seen as a declining number of clergy. At the same time, there have been signs that the global Church is healthier and more confident and vigorous than ever. The papacy – especially under John Paul II and now Francis – has seemingly attracted unprecedented interest and enthusiasm. And while churches were closing in some cities like Montreal, new ones were opening in Toronto and across the West.

Faced with this cacophony of mixed signals and contradictory reports, Reg and I decided to go straight to Catholics to get a more direct reading that would help provide insight into current trends and future directions.

Contrary to dominant views among social scientists that religion has been experiencing a declining role in contemporary societies, we have found precisely the opposite to be the case in Canada when it comes to Catholics. Indeed, globalization and immigration have been bringing to our shores millions of people whose identities are firmly fixed by religious beliefs and practices. Surprisingly, the Catholic Church in Canada is benefiting enormously from developments in the postmodern world that experts had predicted would be its nemesis.

Independent of the immigration factor, we also see a Catholic community that remains deeply rooted in their identity as Catholics. Sure, there are challenges when it comes to increasing levels of participation. But Catholic culture, along with beliefs, practices and the vital role of faith in life's key events – birth, marriage and death – serve to unite the 13 million Canadians who define themselves as Catholic. Our research points to considerable vitality and fertile ground for creating vibrant Christian communities in the new millennium.

Over to Reg...

I don't have much to add to what Angus has written, other than to say that it was a sheer delight to work with him on the important March 2015 survey that has centrally informed this book. Most national surveys have samples in the range of 1,000 to 1,500 cases. When Angus saw the possibility of our doing an analysis of Catholics as part of the study, he immediately increased the sample size to over 3,000 people to ensure Catholics would be adequately represented – doubling his costs in the process. He has made a major contribution to Catholics and to those who want to understand the role of Catholicism in Canadian life by so enthusiastically generating the data.

Another player who added to the positive ambience surrounding this project has been Joseph Sinasac, the Publishing Director at Novalis. From the time we first made contact and told him about the potential book, Joseph and his publishing board have shared our enthusiasm.

The spirit of the research project and this book has been a full-fledged partnership. Angus has taken the lead in producing the data; I have taken the lead in putting the book together. It has been an uplifting and enjoyable relationship.

Our hope is that Catholics and others will find the material to be of value. If our research helps you to see things a bit more clearly and, in the process, your life and faith are elevated, we will feel that our efforts – to paraphrase a well-known song – were not in vain.

Thank you for taking the time to read what we have to say.

1

The Backdrop: The First 500 Years

The Early Centuries

On June 24, 2015, on the feast of Saint John the Baptist, patron saint of French Canadians, more than 2,000 people assembled at Saint-Jean-Baptiste Church on Rachel Street in Montreal. They came to celebrate the 400th anniversary of the first Mass on the island of Montreal, and to commemorate the arrival of the Recollect Franciscans in America.

Contrary to rumour, a strong Catholic pulse continues to beat in Quebec, where it all began.*

* We obviously are offering a brief overview of the history of Catholicism in Canada. Examples of some more detailed accounts include Terence Fay, *A History of Canadian Catholics* (Montreal: McGill-Queen's, 2002); John Webster Grant, *The Church in the Canadian Era* (Vancouver: Regent College, 1998); Terrence Murphy and Roberto Perin, eds., *A Concise History of Christianity in Canada* (Toronto: Oxford, 1996); Mark Noll's brief but thorough essay *What Happened to Christian Canada?* (Vancouver: Regent College, 2007); and Mark McGowan and Solange Lefebvre's excellent overviews of anglophone, allophone and francophone Catholics in Paul Bramadat and David Seljak, eds., *Christianity and Ethnicity in Canada* (Toronto: University of Toronto Press, 2008).

In the Beginning

Catholics have had a long-standing and prominent place in Canadian life. They were among the country's earliest immigrants. Historians tell us that, in all likelihood, the first people to arrive here were Asians who crossed the Bering Strait. They were followed around the year 1000 by the first Europeans, when Vikings from Scandinavia established a short-lived colony on the eastern tip of what is now Newfoundland-Labrador. Catholics weren't far behind.

About 500 years later, in 1497, Italian navigator John Cabot landed on the east coast of "the New World," claiming the land for England, which had commissioned his voyage, while acknowledging the religious authority of the Catholic Church.

> Cabot's arrival was poignant, in that it provided a historical hint of the key to Catholic vitality that remains so important today: immigration.

According to the Canadian Conference of Catholic Bishops, the Church's roots go back to July 7, 1534, when a French priest who had accompanied explorer Jacques Cartier celebrated Mass on the shores of the Gaspé Peninsula.[1] Using an Iroquois word for village (*kanata*), Cartier referred to the general region as "Canada."[2]

> ### The Meeting
>
> On August 1, 1615, subsequent to his arrival in Quebec, de Champlain landed in Penetanguishene Bay, part of what is known today as cottage country north of Toronto. The 400th anniversary of his arrival is remembered in a poignant sculpture by Timothy Schmalz, a Catholic, called *The Meeting*. It depicts the cordial and respectful meeting between two equals – the explorer and Bear Chief Aenon of the Huron Wendat Nation. Champlain is flanked by Jesuit missionaries, Aenon by symbols of the aboriginal creation story. Faith was critical to both parties.
>
> Father Raymond J. de Souza, *National Post*, August 3, 2015.

The settlement of "Quebec" was established in 1608 by Samuel de Champlain, and that first mass on the Island of Montreal was celebrated in 1615. Significantly, France encouraged exploration, settlement and use of the newly discovered lands. The area that stretched deep into what would become the United States became a French colony known as New France in 1663.

In the early 1600s, the first Catholic settlers, the *habitants*, arrived from France. They were followed by Jesuit missionaries and other religious congregations that founded churches and established seminaries. But these Catholics did much more. From the beginning, they recognized the need to address the full scope of life, and proceeded to respond to physical and social needs, open schools and set up hospitals.

For example, when Marie Guenet, Anne Cointre, and Marie Forestier, three sisters of the Augustines Hospitalières, disembarked from their ship at the port of Ville de Québec on August 1, 1639, they brought with them a charter from Louis XVI with a mandate to care for the needs of the sick and disadvantaged in New France. From these humble beginnings, and often under harsh conditions, religious women and men from many religious congregations, along with lay people, carried out this healing ministry across the country for the next 400 years.[3]

Also among these early arrivals was a priest named François de Laval. He arrived in 1659; 15 years later, he became Canada's first bishop, with responsibility for most of Canada and the United States. The early clergy, say historians, had a dream that New France would be a place from which a revitalized Catholicism could spread across North America.[4]

From its earliest days through to the mid-1950s, the Quebec Catholic rural parish was the unit around which communal life revolved. The parish priest, or *curé*, played a powerful leadership role in integrating parish life, and served as the protector and representative of the *habitant*.[5] To this day, a church steeple can be seen in virtually every small town and village in the province.

For close to a century, Canada remained a French and Catholic colony, with a population of about 80,000 in 1750. They included some 10,000 Acadians – descendants of the earliest French settlers, many of whom were Métis – who lived in a territory known as "Acadie" in present-day Nova Scotia and Prince Edward Island.

The British and Protestant Invasion

Battles between Great Britain and France in various parts of the world – including the famous Battle on the Plains of Abraham in Quebec City in 1759 – had important implications for people in the colonies. As France ceded lands to Britain, early Catholics were directly affected. Acadians, for example, were variously banished and deported. However, Britain's Quebec Act of 1774, passed by the British Parliament, guaranteed religious freedom to Roman Catholic colonists, in the course of applying British criminal law and French civil law.

Life for Catholic Colonists in Quebec

The first step in the colonization of Canada was the establishment of the seigniories [land allotments]. They were all about the same size, very narrow and very deep, with frontage along the St. Lawrence or another river.

Each settler built his house at the extreme end of his farm facing the river, not far from that of his neighbour. The Canadian habitant was attached to his land, and he cultivated it unrestrainedly with the help of his family. Near him, other habitants were engaged in a similar enterprise, and this community of interests resulted in a tradition of mutual aid. Apart from family life, neighborly relations were practically the only type of social activity among the Canadian habitants.

The parishes fulfilled the functions of rural municipalities. The Canadian curés [priests] were the real leaders of these communities. It is he who actually controls their social life. It is around him and under him that they gather as a parochial community ... the mentor of his flock – of those he calls his children as they themselves call him their father.

Jean-Charles Falardeau, "The Seventeenth-Century Parish in French Canada," 1976.

The so-called British Conquest, along with the end of the American Revolution in 1776, had two dramatic consequences for the growth of the English presence in Canada and the religious makeup of the emerging country.

First, immigration from France reached a standstill, while Protestant and Catholic migrants from the British Isles came to Canada in increasing numbers. Among them were Irish and Scottish settlers.[6]

Second, with the end of the American Revolution, close to 50,000 United Empire Loyalists made their way to Canada. Some 30,000 settled in the three Maritime provinces, 10,000 in what would become Ontario, and 2,000 or so in the Eastern Townships of present-day Quebec. Around the same time (1778), the first Europeans – led by the English explorers James Cook and George Vancouver – landed on the west coast.

The stage was set for the dominance of Catholics and Protestants. The Catholic Church, far from being passive, made its presence known from the beginnings of "English Canada," establishing dioceses in St. John's in 1784, Charlottetown in 1829, Halifax in 1842, and Victoria in 1846. (Table 1.1)

Table 1.1. Religious Identification: Early 1840s

	Upper Canada 1842	Lower Canada 1844
Roman Catholic	13%	82%
Church of England	22	6
Presbyterian	20	5
Methodist	17	2
Baptist	3	1
Jewish	<1	<1
Other denominations	8	1
No response	17	3

Source: Census of Canada, 1870-71, Vol. 4, Ottawa: 1876. In Kalbach and McVey, 1976:223.

On the way to Confederation, Canada was divided into Lower Canada and Upper Canada in 1791 (the Constitutional Act), with their respective capitals in Quebec and Niagara-on-the-Lake. By 1825, Lower Canada had a population of some 480,000 people and Upper Canada was home to around 160,000, for a total of just under 650,000. The former continued to be heavily Catholic, while the latter was predominantly Protestant.

Fifty years later, with the Act of Union in 1841, the two colonies were merged into the Province of Canada, comprised of Canada East and Canada West. Catholics were given full legal standing. Politics aside, the religious compositions remained unchanged.

Less than three decades later, on July 1, 1867, the Dominion of Canada came into being. The country consisted of Ontario, Quebec, New Brunswick and Nova Scotia. The founding provinces were subsequently joined by Manitoba (1870), British Columbia (1871), Prince Edward Island (1873), Alberta and Saskatchewan (1905) and Newfoundland (1949).

The first Dominion of Canada census of the four original provinces was released in April 1871. It found the population to number about 3.5 million people (1.6 million in Ontario, 1.2 million in Quebec, about 385,000 in Nova Scotia and 285,000 in New Brunswick). Buoyed up by the Loyalists and immigration from Britain, Protestants made up 56% of the overall population; Catholics, 42%. Remarkably, ongoing demographic patterns – immigration and natural increase – would result in the Protestant–Catholic–Other Faith–No Religion patterns remaining fairly steady for almost the next century, through about 1960.

Westward Expansion

The first half of the 19th century also saw the Catholic Church expand into other parts of English Canada. Archdioceses were established, for example, in Kingston (1826), Toronto (1841), Ottawa (1847) and Hamilton (1856). The movement into western and northern Canada was evident, with the establishment of the episcopal district of the Red River in 1820, which in 1871 became the

Archdiocese of Saint-Boniface. A large missionary endeavour was undertaken by the Oblates of Mary Immaculate, particularly among Indigenous peoples.

Following the establishment of the Dominion, the Catholic Church extended its reach to the west coast with the creation of the Vancouver Diocese (1873). Around the same time (1871), the Diocese of St. Albert, embracing greater Edmonton, was founded; the Diocese of Calgary was created four decades later, in 1912. Regina's Diocese came into being around the same time (1911), and the Diocese of Saskatoon appeared two decades later (1933).

In sketching the history of the Catholic Church in Canada, the Canadian Conference of Catholic Bishops explicitly acknowledges that its diversity has been enriched by the presence of Eastern churches. Extensive migration from Eastern Europe in particular has seen the Ukrainian Church, for example, play an important role in the Church's growth, particularly in western Canada.[7]

Catholic Missions in Canada

Since its founding in 1908, Catholic Missions in Canada has come to the aid of isolated missions across the country where a lack of

resources makes it impossible to maintain a Catholic presence without outside financial help. Papal approval and pontifical status were granted by Pope Pius X on June 9, 1910, for "the protection and diffusion of the Catholic Faith in the territories of the Dominion of Canada." In the early days, known then as The Catholic Church Extension Society, it undertook to bring the Church to thousands of Catholics settling in western Canada. It began using funds collected in the east to build small chapels across the prairies and in the mountain areas. Later, it encouraged priests in the Atlantic provinces to go west.

The early work was in response to conditions described in detail by priest George Thomas Daly in 1920. Daly, who served in Saskatchewan before going to the Maritimes, wrote that the obstacles of geography, ethnicity and the absence of Catholic tradition "are the ever open crevices through which a tremendous leakage

→

has been draining the vitality of the Church in Western Canada. So the call of the West is like the frantic S.O.S. on the high seas. It is the cry of thousands of Catholics sinking into the sea of unbelief and irreligion. Has the Church in the East heard it? What is the response?"

Catholic Missions in Canada: www.cmic.info; George Thomas Daly, *Catholic Problems in Western Canada*, 1921:7.

The 19th and 20th Centuries

From the 1860s to 1960s

In the century spanning the creation of the Dominion and the 1960s, religious identification remained pervasive across the country. As noted, it is telling that the proportions of Catholics, Protestants and individuals adhering to Other Faiths changed little over the period. People who acknowledged that they had "no religion" were so few in number that the census takers essentially disregarded them. Between 1931 and 1961, the proportion of Catholics increased by about five percentage points, at the expense of Protestants, whose market share decreased by close to the same number. (Figure 1.1)

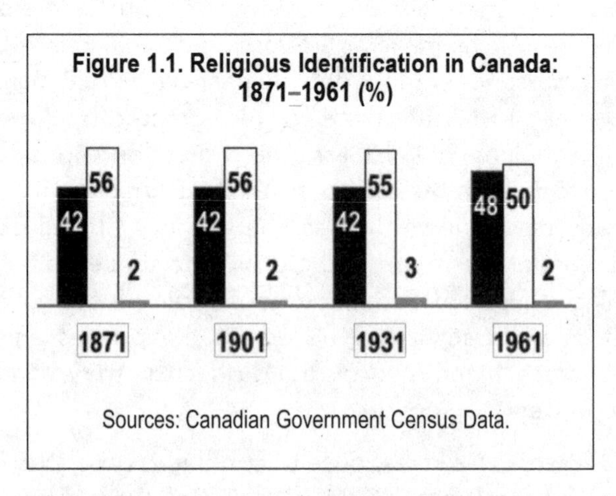

Those kinds of percentages appear flat. But, particularly for Catholics and Protestants, these percentages were associated with significant numerical increases, as the Canadian population grew from 3.2 million in 1861 to 7.2 million in 1911 and to 18.2 million by 1961. (Table 1.2)

Table 1.2. Catholic Expansion by Province: 1871–1971
(In 1000s)

	1871	1911	1931	1951	1971
TOTALS	**1,532**	**2,833**	**4,285**	**6,069**	**9,975**
Quebec	1,020	1,725	2,462	3,564	5,227
Ontario	274	485	745	1,142	2,569
Nova Scotia	102	145	163	218	286
New Brunswick	96	145	188	261	331
PE Island	40	42	39	44	51
Saskatchewan	---	90	234	199	259
Manitoba	---	74	190	156	243
Alberta	---	62	168	186	391
British Columbia	---	58	91	168	408
Territories	---	7	5	8	19
Newfoundland	---	---	---	122	191

Sources: Statistics Canada Census Data.

- During this hundred-year period, Catholic numbers jumped from about 1.5 million in 1871 to some 10 million by 1971 – in Quebec alone, Catholics increased from about 1 million to more than 5 million.
- As of the end of the 1960s, Catholics continued to constitute an overwhelming majority in Quebec and close to half of the populations of New Brunswick and Prince Edward Island. Elsewhere, Catholics made up one third to one quarter of the provincial populations, with their market share a bit lower at 20% in British Columbia.

A major factor in the growth of the population was, of course, immigration. In the early part of the 20th century, Canadian immigration levels soared, topping 400,000 in 1913 – before falling as the First World War began in 1914. Soon after the war ended in 1919, the levels began to climb again – slipping once more with the Great Depression of the 1930s and the outbreak of the Second World War in 1939. From the end of the war in 1945 through the 1960s, figures again were on the rise. (Table 1.3)

Table 1.3. Total Immigration to Canada: 1860–1965
In 1000s

Year	Immigration	Year	Immigration
1860	6	**1950**	74
1870	25	**1951**	194
1880	39	**1952**	164
1890	75	**1953**	169
1900	42	**1954**	154
1910	287	**1955**	110
1913	401	**1956**	165
1915	37	**1957**	282
1920	139	**1958**	125
1930	105	**1959**	107
1940	11	**1960**	104
1945	23	**1965**	147

Source: Statistics Canada.

The arrival of large numbers of "ready-made" Catholics through the immigration pipeline was a bonanza for the Church. Typically younger than their Canadian counterparts, they injected numbers, vitality and diversity into dioceses across the country.

Of considerable importance, the historical evidence suggests that Catholic leaders and other church leaders were well aware of the needs and potential contributions of the new arrivals. As a result, many were well prepared for their arrival.

As the 1970s began, about 50% of Canadians were Catholic. Some 6 in 10 had French origins, including about 85% of Catholics in Quebec.

But reflecting the arrival of Catholics from other European countries, the remaining 4 in 10 in the rest of the country had different roots. (Table 1.4)

Table 1.4. National Backgrounds of Catholics: 1931 and 1971

	1931	1971		
	ALL	ALL	Quebec	ROC
TOTAL	**41%**	**48%**	**84%**	**30%**
French	**66**	**59**	**86**	**23**
British Isles	**16**	**18**	**06**	**35**
English	*04*	---	---	---
Irish	*09*	---	---	---
Scottish	*03*	---	---	---
Other	*<1*	---	---	---
Other European	**16**	**17**	**06**	**32**
Ukrainian	*04*	*01*	*<1*	*02*
German	*03*	*03*	*01*	*06*
Polish	*03*	*02*	*01*	*04*
Italian	*02*	*08*	*04*	*14*
Netherlands	*<1*	*01*	*<1*	*02*
Other	*04*	*02*	*<1*	*04*
Indigenous	**02**	**01**	**<1**	**02**
Other	**<1**	**04**	**02**	**08**

Sources: Statistics Canada Census Data.

Almost 70% of Catholics outside Quebec had British (35%) or other European backgrounds (32%), led by people from Italy, Germany, Poland, Ukraine and the Netherlands. Adding to the diversity of Catholicism, another 2% of Canada's Catholics had Indigenous origins. Those background variations were particularly apparent in the makeup of parishes. For Catholic administrators, such diversity made for a difficult juggling act when it came to establishing and staffing parishes and dioceses.

Work among immigrants of nationalities other than British or French

Work among immigrants of nationalities other than British or French called for new approaches by all churches. The first need was to welcome them to Canada and to help them to establish themselves. Most denominations maintained chaplains at ports of entry. Neil McNeil, Roman Catholic archbishop of Vancouver from 1910 to 1912, set up a Catholic Immigrants' Information Office in that city. At Winnipeg a Catholic Immigrant Aid Society was under the direction of the Oblates, who despite their generally French orientation were tireless in their efforts to reach newcomers. By the beginning of the first war most churches had established regular procedures for meeting immigrants and helping them through their initial period of adjustment.

John Webster Grant in *The Church in the Canadian Era,* 1988:95.

Involvement and Importance

The pervasive perception is that the century spanning the 1860s through the 1960s was a time when religion was highly valued by Catholics and pretty much everyone else. People attended religious services in large numbers. Faith had an impact on personal and collective life.

We do not have a lot of good hard data on levels of actual participation. But we can readily offer some familiar and informative qualitative and quantitative illustrations.

The Catholic Women's League

The Catholic Women's League was organized nationally in 1920 and incorporated in 1923. It is officially recognized by the Canadian Conference of Catholic Bishops as a lay association of women and is affiliated with the World Union of Catholic Women's Organizations (WUCWO) which in turn has consultative ties with United Nations agencies.

→

The CWL serves to unite Canadian Catholic women and pursue goals that include individual and spiritual development, promotion of Catholic teachings, living out the Christian ideal in home and family life, enhancing the role of women in church and society, and contributing to social justice, freedom, and peace.

The league's national office is in Winnipeg. It currently has close to 100,000 members in 1,300 parish based councils. The CWL also has diocesan, provincial, regional, and national councils. Local groups typically meet about once a month. National assemblies take place annually. The League functions as an important resource to local Catholic parishes, and well beyond.

Catholic Women's League websites: http://cwl.ca and www.cwltoronto.ca.

- Mark Twain, in a famous speech at a banquet in his honour in Montreal on December 8, 1881, commented, "This is the first time I was ever in a city where you couldn't throw a brick without breaking a church window. Yet I was told that you were going to build one more. I said the scheme is good, but where are you going to find room? They said, we will build it on top of another church and use an elevator."[8]

Catholic identity and ethnic loyalties

Since being Catholic was and is often closely associated with ethnic loyalties, the Church had to face the formidable problems of coordinating the various old world allegiances. Catholic bishops generally managed to juggle personnel and building requirements. When a specific ethnic group was sufficiently large, bishops often promoted an ethnic parish for the area. When numbers did not warrant such an expense, they often attached Polish, Italian, Lithuanian and other priests to local parishes, encouraged in the old world language.

By combining foreign and English masses in one parish, the hierarchy also kept a hold on the younger generation, which too often tended to become disenchanted with the un-Canadian (as they thought) parental tradition.

→

In later years, matching settlers and bishops of the same ethnic origin proved to be less easy. This was particularly true of western Canada. French Canadians became a decreasing minority, yet the bishops remained French. Against the advice of the French archbishop, the Vatican appointed an Irishman to the Diocese of Calgary in 1912. Meanwhile, in Winnipeg, the English and French groups remained at loggerheads, and so in 1916 the Pope decided to divide the Archdiocese of St. Boniface and appointed an Irish prelate to the new Archdiocese of Winnipeg. One Irish priest was appointed to the Archdiocese in 1921 and another one to Regina in 1929.

"English Catholicism," in Hans Mol, *Faith and Fragility*, 1985:203-204.

- In 1945, Gallup conducted what is believed to be the first national survey of attendance. What the pollster found was that 65% of Canadians had attended a service in the three-week period after Easter – a level that was higher than that in the United States. While variations in the release are sketchy, Gallup reported that the highest provincial level was found in Quebec, where Catholics made up a 95% majority: there, 9 in 10 people said they had attended a service during the post-Easter period.
- Gallup's polling of people who had attended a service "in the previous seven days" found the national Catholic figure to be 83% in 1946, 87% in 1956%, and 83% as late as 1965. So it was that the legendary Cardinal Léger could offer this much-cited observation about the religiosity level in Montreal in the late 1950s: "At seven every night, Montreal would be kneeling, saying the Rosary with me."[9]

Beyond attendance, by most accounts, Catholics – and Protestants as well – knew the influence of religion in life during the 1860s to 1960s period.

Having Their Own Schools

Having their own schools has always been extremely important to Catholics. Along with the parish and family, schools have been viewed as an essential component in creating Catholic community, instilling faith and values, and interpreting and living out life. So it is that Catholic schools – often described as "separate schools" – date back to early 17th-century Quebec, and spread across the country with emerging Catholic parishes.

With Confederation and the BNA Act in 1867, support of Catholic and Protestant school systems was enshrined. Over time, most Protestant systems have evolved into public systems. However, full funding for Catholic schools has continued through today in Ontario, Alberta, Saskatchewan and the Territories. In addition, the four western provinces, along with Manitoba, Quebec and the Territories, offer partial funding to Catholic and other religious schools that meet certain criteria. The Atlantic provinces stand alone in providing no funding for religious schools. Ontario provides funding – full funding – for Catholic schools only.

An Illustrative List of Canadian Catholic Schools

1663	Laval, Québec City Originally
1802	Saint Mary's, Halifax
1852	St. Michael's, Toronto
1853	St. Francis Xavier, Antigonish
1865	St. Jerome's, Waterloo
1873	Mount Saint Vincent
1890	Université Sainte-Anne, Nova Scotia
1910	St. Thomas, Fredericton
1917	Campion, Regina
1919	University of Montreal Originally
1919	Brescia, London
1926	St. Joseph's, Edmonton
1936	St. Thomas More, Saskatoon
1956	St. Mark's, Vancouver
1965	Saint Paul, Ottawa
2004	St. Mary's, Calgary

Through the 1950s, the Catholic Church seems to have had considerable input into the life of Quebec and lives of Quebeckers. In rural areas, as noted earlier, local priests knew a high level of influence over personal and community life. In urban areas as well, social organizations and social institutions were fused with the Church. Quebec playwright Jacques Godbout, in a blunt, unflattering assessment, has written that through the late 1950s, the Roman Catholic Church maintained "a stranglehold on Quebec society, controlled social life from birth to death, ran schools and hospitals, censored the press and kept a tight lid on the intellectual and artistic pot."[10] As Gregory Baum has succinctly put it, through the end of the 1950s, the Church's organizational presence was ubiquitous and its cultural power enormous.[11]

In the rest of Canada, the vast majority of Catholics also attended mass with regularity well into the 1960s. (Table 1.5) Most appear to have held traditional attitudes about marriage, Lent and celibacy, as well as conventional beliefs concerning God, the divinity of Jesus, and life after death. They relied on the Church for key rites of passage related to birth, marriage and death.

Table 1.5. Some Indicators of Catholic Religiosity: 1940–1970

Select Gallup Poll Items

	Canada	RCs	Prots
1942			
Divorce in this country is too easy to get: *agree*	27%	42%	20%
1946			
Attended a service in the previous seven days	67	83	60
1955			
Religion is having a greater influence in Canadian life	53	56	50
Women: favour word "obey" in marriage ceremony	43	49	38
Usually give up something during Lent	37	78	12
1957			
Attended a service in the previous seven days	60	87	43
1968			
Churches should be involved in political/social matters	52	52	52
1967			
Roman Catholic priests should be allowed to marry	68	46	72
1969			
Believe in God	92	97	90
Believe in Heaven	72	86	66
Believe in Hell	40	52	33

The Canadian Conference of Catholic Bishops

The CCCB is the national assembly of the Bishops of Canada. It was founded in 1943 and officially recognized by the Holy See in 1948. After the Second Vatican Council (1962-65) the CCCB became part of a worldwide network of Episcopal Conferences, established in 1965, as an integral part of the life of the universal Church. Until 1977, it was called the Canadian Catholic Conference. The change in name reflects more clearly the fact that it is an association of Bishops.

According to the statutes of the CCCB, the Bishops together exercise some pastoral functions for Catholics in Canada, while respecting the autonomy of each Bishop in the service of his particular Church. Through the work of its members, the Conference is involved in matters of national and international scope in areas such as ecumenism and interfaith dialogue, theology, social justice, aid to developing countries, the protection of human life, liturgy, communications and Christian education. The Conference also provides the Bishops with a forum where they can share their experience and insights on the life of the Church and the major events that shape our society.

Source: CCCB website: www.cccb.ca.

By all accounts, most Catholics valued faith and took seriously the need to apply the teachings of the Church to everyday life.

In 1985, McMaster University religious studies expert Hans Mol summed up the Catholic presence in life this way: "Throughout its long history, the Catholic Church has been the prime defender of national solidarity, communal integrity, family cohesion, and personality integration in French Canada."[12] In the rest of Canada, as well, he writes, the Church attempted not only to have a strong impact on the lives of individuals but also on collective life more generally. "It has taken its service function to society, community, and family very seriously," he wrote, pursuing social justice and establishing a large number of orphanages, hospitals and homes for the aged. Education was another top priority.[13] Through the end of the 1950s, the influence of the Catholic Church was everywhere.

The Catholic Church and Indigenous Peoples

Throughout the 17th century many Catholic missionaries dedicated their lives to minister to Indigenous peoples [showing] great concern for [their] spiritual and human welfare.

The tradition of Catholic service was carried north and west. It is exemplified by the commitment of the Oblates of Mary Immaculate in their ministry to the people of the Northwest and the Arctic. Father Albert Lacombe ... Bishop Vital-Justin Grandin ... the Grey Nuns ... are prominent examples among the many Catholics, Indigenous and non-Indigenous, who have served and continue to serve in hospitals, schools and other forms of social services.

Today Catholics, like other Canadians, are becoming more aware of how their relationships with Indigenous peoples have often been marked by imperialism and colonialism. ... If there were bishops and missionaries championing aboriginal rights, there were also theologians and Church leaders defending colonial exploitations. While some missionaries attempted to protect and understand native cultures, others failed to value nation beliefs and customs as seeds of the Word of God. It must be acknowledged that the missionary endeavor was deeply marked by the prevailing attitudes of the superiority of European culture.

Despite these struggles, the Church has walked with Aboriginal Peoples, shared their joys, their sufferings, and their aspirations. Then and now, the Churches provide a place where Native and non-Native Peoples may find common ground.

Source: CCCB website, 2015: www.cccb.ca. Selected highlights.

And Then It All Seemed to Collapse

In Quebec and elsewhere, the reality of urbanization between the 1860s and 1960s had major implications for the Church's impact on the lives of individual Catholics. Between 1871 and 1971, the percentage of Canadians living in communities of more than 1,000 people increased from 20% to 76%. In Quebec, the figures jumped from 12% in 1871 to 80% in 1971. The days of Quebec's Catholics being predominantly rural *habitants* linked by their parishes belonged to the past. The same was true of Catholics living in the rest of the country.

"By the end of the 1960s," wrote respected historian John Webster Grant, "all indicators of participation in church activities were heading downward at an alarming and accelerating rate." He added, "The crisis was felt most severely in Quebec, where adherence to the Roman Catholic Church has from time immemorial been an accepted fact of life."[14] In the words of journalist Konrad Yakabuski (2009), attendance in Quebec "didn't so much collapse as vaporize – at least among those born after 1945."[15]

Those same Gallup polls that had documented the high level of attendance through the 1960s led the way in documenting the sharp decline in service attendance from the 1960s onward. (Table 1.6) The Protestant participation declines were evident by around 1950, with Catholics following suit in the late 1960s.

Table 1.6. Service Attendance for Catholics and Protestants: 1946–1998

*"Did you yourself happen to go to church or synagogue in the last seven days?"**

	1946	1956	1965	1975	1985	1998
Roman Catholics	83%	87%	83%	61%	43%	36%
Protestants	60	43	32	25	29	32
ALL OF CANADA	67	61	55	41	32	29

**1998: "a place of worship."*

Source: Canadian Institute of Public Opinion/Gallup Canada.

Apart from sheer attendance, religion's influence also declined sharply in the post-1950s. In Quebec, a reflection of the tenor of the times could be seen in the election of the Liberal government of Jean Lesage in 1960, with one of its prominent slogans being "It's time for a change." What ensued very quickly was the Quiet Revolution and the conscious effort to modernize the province.

As part of what some have dubbed "the Quieter Revolution," the Catholic Church relinquished control over the majority of its schools, hospitals and social service institutions.[16] As Montreal historian Claude Bélanger has put it, "The increasing involvement of the Church in all aspects of the life of French Canadians contained the germs of the demise of Church influence: the Church was unable to finance all these institutions and to provide the personnel to support them." The result was the recognition that the State had to take over many of these responsibilities.[17] In the process, the Church's influence in the economic and political spheres was largely muted.

But much more was happening than urbanization and overextension. Gregory Baum has written that Quebeckers "wanted to catch up with modern society, be open to pluralism, participate in democratic decision making, express themselves in art and literature free of censorship, and create a modern educational system qualifying students to advance in the fields of science and technology." He adds that they "also wanted to free themselves from the economic domination of the English-Canadian elite and assume full political responsibility for their own society."[18]

Accompanying the structural changes was a multi-faceted shift in outlook, summed up well by a group of bishops in their report to Rome in 1974: a traditional society had given way to "a pluralistic, segmented, declericalized, secularized, permissive, industrialized, and urbanized society."[19] One public symbol was the fact that the major celebration of French Canadian nationhood on June 24 changed from being Catholic, in the form of St. Jean Baptiste Day, to the secular La Fête Nationale.

In short, as David Seljak has put it, "The rapidity with which secularization overtook Quebec society and political culture was staggering."[20]

Abuse and the Decline in Confidence

In Canada, attention was particularly focused on the Mount Cashel orphanage in Newfoundland, schools operated by Christian Brothers in towns near Toronto, Quebec's "Orphans of Duplessis," group homes in Saskatchewan, and the Prince George Diocese in British Columbia. In addition, there were widespread

→

accusations of decades of mistreatment of Aboriginal children who were attending residential schools. Between 1985 and 1990, the percentage of Canadians expressing high levels of confidence in religious leaders dropped from 51% to 37% – in the Atlantic region from 74% to 40%. In the case of Catholics, confidence fell from 62% to 47%.

Reginald W. Bibby, *Unknown Gods*, 1993:68–75.

The problems of organized religion in both Canada and the United States were exacerbated in the 1980s and early '90s by a significant loss of confidence as a result of a series of scandals and revelations of sexual abuse. Allegations, charges and convictions spread like an epidemic.

Yet, remarkably, survey findings showed that the decrease in the confidence of religious leaders did not, by itself, result in lower attendance or the bypassing of rites of passage. Large numbers of Catholics and other Canadians demonstrated a surprising amount of resilience and patience.[21] For many, faith was seemingly more important than less-than-perfect leaders.

As the 20th century wound down, the Catholic Church in Quebec that had, like its 17th-century founders, sought to encompass all of life seemed to have been relegated to the margins of everyday life. It still had a voice and still could make declarations and presentations and aspire to play something of a prophetic observer role.[22] But it increasingly appeared to be only one voice among many, its unique role in the life of the province limited primarily to administering the Eucharist and performing rites of passage.[23] And rather than all of Montreal kneeling to say the Rosary, Quebec's weekly mass attendance had plummeted from 88% in 1957 to about 25% by 2000.

But the Catholic attendance dropoff was not limited to Quebec. In the rest of Canada, weekly Catholic numbers also had declined significantly – from 75% in 1957 to around 45% by the end of the century.[24] Beyond only attendance, it also seemed apparent that there was a significant drop in the Church's influence in individual Catholic lives. Grant alludes to the magnitude of that drop when he notes that Protestant denominations "had never been able to command the active participation of all members of their constituencies" to the extent that the Catholic Church did – and consequently the Protestants "did not have so far to fall."[25]

The main factors transforming Catholicism were similar to those found in much of the modern world. Industrialization and post-industrialization tend to place strict limits on the areas of life over which religion has authority. That process, of course, has come to be referred to as secularization. Two of its foremost characteristics are institutional specialization and, for individuals, selective consumption – or what the French call *religion à la carte*.

An Important Effort at Renewal – Vatican II

The Second Vatican Council, commonly known as "Vatican II," was convened in Rome by Pope John XXIII in 1962 and lasted through December of 1965. The primary goal of the Council was the modernization and updating ("aggiornamento") of the Roman Catholic Church. Among the changes: celebration of mass in the vernacular; relaxing of Friday dietary guidelines and discarding of nuns' habits; greater participation by the people in hymns and responses; revised catechisms; increased "dialogue" with other disciplines and other religions; greater consultation of leaders and laity – including women – in the governing of the Church.

A 1986 bishops' national survey of Canadian Catholics found that 86% felt the changes were mostly for the better. On the plus side, Catholics cited liturgy in the language of the people and greater participation of the laity; on the minus side, some mentioned the downplaying of doctrine, moral demands, and popular devotions. (Bibby 1987:17–18)

Thomas Groome comments that "for a few, the Council went too far, making Catholicism indistinguishable from liberal Protestantism." But, "for many more, the spirit of Vatican II has been compromised. And for a whole generation of young people," he continues, "it's like Woodstock, something from the sixties." (Groome 2003: xx–xxi)

The Current Situation

As Canada moved into the 21st century, the dominant mood across the country was one of gloom and doom for religion. The Protestant Mainline – the United Church, Anglicans, Lutherans and Presbyterians – were all experiencing fairly dramatic declines in participation and revenues. The golden days of the 1950s and '60s were relegated to the memories of the older stalwarts and were largely unknown to those who were younger.

In Quebec in particular, morale was low among large numbers of leaders and parishioners. But the story of decline, decay and demoralization was being widely told and widely felt by other Catholics and Canadians in other parts of Canada. Secularization, it seemed, was now rampant everywhere. Things were bad, and they would only get worse.

Places where there was life and growth were treated as temporary anomalies. Like aging and death, it would only be a matter of time before they likewise would experience what most observers viewed as the inevitable impact of secularization. Calls to be "faithful remnants," "significant minorities," "prevailing churches" and the like were common. They hardly inspired the troops.

Where was hope when people needed it?

2

New Life in the 21st Century

Putting Things into Perspective

The primary reason that we wanted you to wade through our first chapter is because of a strong bias that both of us have. We believe that to make sense of life in Canada, including religious developments, we have to put things into perspective – historically and globally. Otherwise, we risk becoming focused on ourselves and our own idiosyncrasies, and are unable to locate what is happening in the here and now within the larger historical and global pictures.

Comparisons with the Americans

When we look at the decline in Catholic and Protestant participation that took place between the 1960s and 2000, it is easy to have no perspective at all. Indeed, many observers simply compared figures in that period with the much-cited Gallup figure from 1945, when something like 85% of Catholics were allegedly attending services every week. As for global perspective, the usual tactic was at best for onlookers to compare Canadian developments with what was taking place in the United States – despite the fact that apart from geographical proximity and access to some illustrative data, there was little reason to do so.

Obviously, attendance in Canada was down significantly from the 1950s and '60s. (Table 2.1) The near-unanimous conclusion of observers? If Gallup was correct in charting ongoing high attendance levels in the U.S. during this time when Canadian attendance was plunging, what further evidence was needed to convince everybody that religion "up here" was in big trouble? And why did we have any reason not to believe that the worst was yet to come?

Table 2.1. Attendance for Catholics & Protestants: U.S.A., 1955–1998

*"Did you yourself happen to go to church or synagogue in the last seven days?"**

	1955	1967	1975	1985	1998
ALL	49%	43%	40%	42%	40%
Roman Catholics	74	66	54	52	44
Protestants	42	39	38	39	44

Source: The Gallup Poll 2003, 2004.

To be honest, many of us who made Canadian–American comparisons weren't typically very precise. It's true that Gallup reported that U.S. attendance as a whole remained fairly stable at around 40% during the last half of the 20th century – something that many of us emphasized. A closer look at American attendance patterns shows that Catholic attendance "down there" actually fell significantly, from approximately 75% in 1955 to about 45% by the end of the century.

But guess what? That drop for the 1 in 4 Americans who viewed themselves as Catholic[1] was *almost exactly the same as it was for the 1 in 4 Canadian Catholics outside Quebec* during the same time period! Presumably, some of the same factors affecting American Catholics were affecting their Canadians counterparts "up here" as well. (Figure 2.1) That parallel finding for Catholics in both Canada and the U.S. warranted some thoughtful analyses. We are not aware that they have ever been carried out.

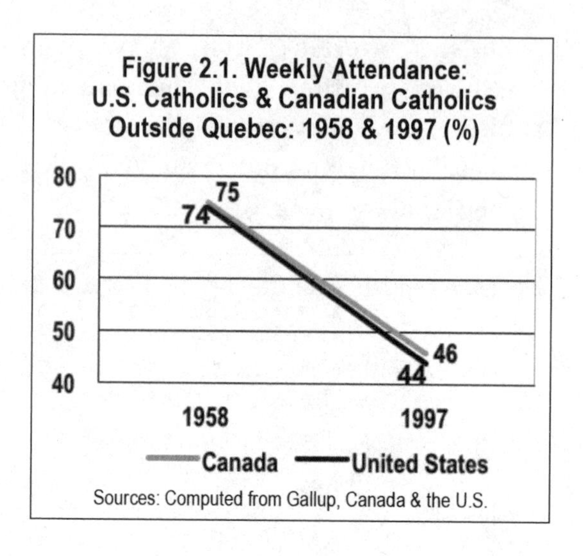

Figure 2.1. Weekly Attendance: U.S. Catholics & Canadian Catholics Outside Quebec: 1958 & 1997 (%)

Sources: Computed from Gallup, Canada & the U.S.

Comparisons with the Europeans

For those who wanted to look further for geographical comparisons, the logical place for many observers to take their cues was Europe. Academic proclamations offered by a core of well-known, predominantly 19th-century thinkers led by the likes of Auguste Comte, Emile Durkheim, Karl Marx and Sigmund Freud seemingly provided an explanatory window for what was taking place in Canada. They have since been joined by many contemporary thinkers.[2]

Put succinctly, these prominent thinkers have maintained that religion was something people turned to in the past to cope with existence. But as our collective civilization moved forward, there would no longer be a need to rely on religion. People in advanced societies would draw on a superior way of thinking in the form of science (Comte), be less inclined to fill the gaps of the unknown by relying on the supernatural (Durkheim), put an end to undesirable and oppressive conditions (Marx), and live life and face death with no illusions of either heavenly hope or supernatural help (Freud). Contemporaries are less strident, but still see the decline of religion as primarily linear-like and irreversible.

Reflecting the Times

These thinkers were writing from experience: for the most part, the immediate experience of Europe and particularly France. The historically dominant Catholic Church was in decline. As Durkheim put it, "We are going through a stage of transition and moral mediocrity. The great things of the past which filled our fathers with enthusiasm do not excite the same ardour in us. In a word, the old gods are growing old or already dead, and others are not yet born."

Emile Durkheim, *The Elementary Forms of the Religious Life*, 1965:475.

And so it was that those of us in the social sciences in Canada were taught what we then proceeded to pass on to our post-1960s students – that what was happening here was something that had already taken place in much of Europe and other advanced places around the world.

- As societies move forward, they increasingly rely on *science* to make sense of life.
- The perspective is characterized by *a secularization of consciousness* at the individual level – we see life and how it unfolds through naturalistic rather than religious eyes.
- With greater levels of education also comes the *specialization of institutions* – the growing ability to make use of an array of institutions to deal with spheres of activity – industry, politics, education, health care, social services, leisure, entertainment and so on. That kind of institutional specialization is a far cry from the old, Church-led social organization of life in rural Quebec in days gone by. It also is very different from the Church-led organization and influence on life found in many other parts of Canada in the 18th and 19th centuries.
- And *religious organizations* themselves become much like other organizations – using many similar criteria, including measures of success, to evaluate their effectiveness.[3]

In short, a number of prominent European thinkers provided us with a set of glasses that we used to explain what was occurring in Canada. Catholics and Protestants here were sharing in a reality that is virtually inevitable in all advanced societies. Religion loses influence over individuals and societies in a fairly linear, one-directional manner. The explanatory perspective? *Secularization*.

But it turns out that what we were telling our students and other people was not particularly accurate. While the secularization thesis clearly has some explanatory value in some places, it is not always a good lens for understanding the role religion plays in the life of societies and the lives of individuals. The secularization glass slipper, we believe, is not a very good fit for Canada.

If the use of the thesis had been restricted to discussions in classrooms and between academics, the costs of its limitations would have been minor. The problem was that secularization was so widely trumpeted and adopted that it became part of the mindset of most religious leaders and others who valued faith.

As a result, this faulty view of the religious sky falling was not merely inaccurate – something of a debate between academics. It also was not very helpful for religious leaders who were attempting to interpret the times and develop effective policy and program responses.

Even more seriously, the secularization view of developments in many instances had a demoralizing and debilitating impact on those who valued faith and were involved in the life of churches. Why try to move forward when religion and churches do not have futures? "Faithful minorities" who are resigned to their finite futures hardly attract new people, new resources and new energy.

Through about 2000, our students were getting "A's" for mastering the secularization interpretation of Canadian religious trends. Today, students are receiving "A's" for a very different reading of things.

The Sky Didn't Fall

It was as if the devastating storm that the weather forecaster said was on the way never arrived. Sure, there was quite a bit of rain and, yes, some of houses – particularly those of the Mainline Protestants, led by the United, Anglican, Presbyterian and Lutheran churches – were pretty badly damaged, as was the Catholic Church in Quebec.

But elsewhere, religion was far from obliterated. Three things were readily apparent in the first decade of the new century.

Ongoing Identification

First, for all the talk about the decline of organized religion, the 2001 census served to remind us that the vast majority of people in the country – some 85% – continued to identify with one group or another. Just 16% of Canadians said they had no religion. Some groups were losing ground, but others were taking over their market shares. As of 2001, there were just about as many Muslims as Lutherans, and Buddhist numbers were closing in on Presbyterians. The religious landscape was shifting, but religion was hardly disappearing.

Polarization

Second, beyond sheer religious identification, it also was clear from just about everyone's polls that *a solid core of people were continuing to embrace religion*, precisely at a time when considerable media attention was being given to *an increasing number of people who seemed to be rejecting it*. In between the two polar opposites, a sizable number of Canadians were neither embracing nor rejecting religion. They seemed to be showing up for services every once in a while, and holding onto a wide variety of beliefs about things like God and life after death. They also were indicating that they were doing things like praying privately at least occasionally, and acknowledging in large numbers their reliance on religious groups for funerals, weddings and birth-related ceremonies.

One general indicator of these inclinations to variously embrace, reject and be ambivalent toward religion was service attendance. As of 2005, for example, about 1 in 3 Canadians were indicating that they were attending a service once a month or more, just under 1 in 3 said they were showing up several times a year through about once a year, and just over 1 in 3 reported that they never attend services. (Figure 2.2)

Figure 2.2. Canadian Service Attendance: 2005 (%)

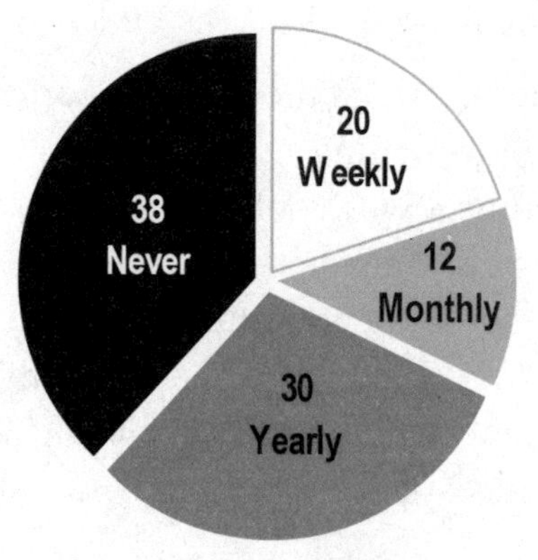

Source: 2005 General Social Survey.

These kinds of variations in the posture toward religion pointed not to a society where religion was increasingly giving way to no religion – in keeping with the *secularization* argument. On the contrary, the choices pointed to *polarization*. Some people continued to value religion, some did not, and many were making up an ambivalent middle.

These three inclinations constitute a continuum. The positions are not fixed and final. Rather, the balance is dynamic and potentially ever-changing, in keeping with any number of personal and social factors, including the activities of religious groups. (Figure 2.3)

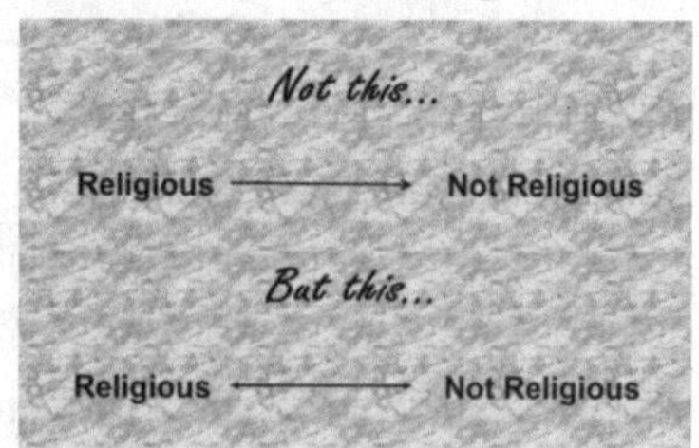

Source: 2005 General Social Survey

Figure 2.3. The Polarization Continuum

Religious	Ambivalent	Not Religious

Source: Reginald Bibby, *Beyond the Gods & Back*, 2011:56.

Worldwide Religious Vitality

The third thing that was readily apparent early in the 21st century – in addition to ongoing identification and polarization – was the potential for immigration, as in the past, to transform the religious situation in Canada once again.

Near the end of the first decade of the new century, word was coming in from religious demographers that globally, religion was experiencing considerable vitality, pointing to ongoing life and even resurgence. Christianity and Islam were leading the way in unprecedented levels of worldwide religious growth.

Newsflash!

RELIGION MAKING A GLOBAL COMEBACK

- Christianity and Islam are the fastest-growing religions
- Christianity is on its biggest roll in its 2,000-year history
  its numbers and market share are at all-time highs
- 1950–2000: Catholics grew from 500 million to over 1 billion
- 1900–2000: Pentecostals grew from zero to half a billion
- key growth regions: Africa, Asia, Latin America
- by 2050: could be 220 million Christians in China – 15% of population

Source: Reginald W. Bibby, *Beyond the Gods & Back*, 2011:202–203.

- In the 20th century, Catholic numbers increased from 266 million in 1900 to 1.1 billion in 2000, and total 1.2 billion today.[4]
- As of 2000, Islam had some 1.5 billion followers.
- The upstart Pentecostals increased from virtually zero in 1900 to half a billion people by the end of the century.
- Growth was particularly pronounced in regions such as Africa, Asia and Latin America, with future growth projected for countries including China.
- A Catholic Church membership was 75% European and North American in 1900. Today, close to 70% of Catholics reside in Africa, Asia and Latin America. To a degree never before experienced, Catholic leadership is beginning to come from all over the world.[5]
- The Pew Research Center recently confirmed the high global numbers. Pew found that as of 2010, 84% of people worldwide were identifying with a religious group. The highly publicized "unaffiliated" or "no religion" figure was lagging well behind at 16%. (Table 2.2)

Table 2.2. Religious Group Numbers Worldwide, 2010

In Millions

1. Christians	2,168	31%
2. Muslims	1,600	23
3. Unaffiliated	1.131	16
4. Hindus	1,032	15
5. Buddhists	488	7
6. Folk Religions	405	6
7. Jews	14	<1
8. Other Religions	58	1

Source: Pew Research Center 2015:8.

The Global Take of a Prominent Observer

Contrary to the constant predictions that religion is doomed, there is abundant evidence of an ongoing worldwide religious awakening. Never before have four out of five people on earth claimed to belong to one of the great world faiths.

Today there are millions of devout Protestants in Latin America – not so long ago there were none. Even so, Latin American Catholics are far more religious than ever before. Sub-Saharan Africa is now home to more church-going Christians than anywhere else on earth, and North Africa and the Middle East are ablaze with Muslim fervor. Hinduism has never been stronger and India's transport systems are straining to meet the demands of pilgrims. The Chinese have rebuilt tens of thousands of temples destroyed by the Red Guards and millions have converted to Christianity.

The world is not merely as religious as it used to be. In important ways, it is far *more* intensely religious than ever before; indeed, it is far more churched. Although the details often differ from place to place, the story remains much the same: the temples, mosques, pagodas, chapels, and churches are full, and even most people who do not attend say they are religious.

Rodney Stark, *The Triumph of Faith*, 2015, Kindle location (K) 4152, 172.

The Immigration Windfall for Religion in Canada

Sociologists work from the assumption that we never are islands unto ourselves – as individuals or as countries. We always are influenced by our broader social environments. Nationally, that means that what happens in Canada will, to a large extent, depend on what is taking place in the rest of the world.

As we all know well – and as was underlined in the first chapter – Canada has always been shaped extensively by immigration. The Catholic Church is a prime example.

At this point in Canadian history, we are facing a serious demographic crisis. The Baby Boomers, who were born in unprecedented numbers between approximately 1945 and 1965, are now in their 50s, 60s and 70s. As they disappear from the Canadian scene, we will not have enough births to offset their deaths.

After 2030: The Central Role of Immigration in Population Growth

Between 1851 and 2001, natural increase was the main factor behind Canada's population growth. The proportion of growth due to natural increase, however, has declined since the late 1960s. Since 2001, it has accounted for about one-third of population growth.

According to all scenarios used in Statistics Canada's most recent population projections, natural increase is expected to continue to decline in the future decades, due to a projected increase in the number of deaths. The aging of the population will accelerate between 2011 and 2031 as baby boomers reach the age of 65. In 2026, the first of the baby boomers will reach the age of 80, an age when mortality is high. As a result, the number of deaths will increase significantly.

Starting in 2031, migratory increase could account for more than 80% of Canada's population growth, compared to about 67% currently. Without a sustained level of immigration or a substantial increase in fertility, Canada's population growth could, within 20 years, be close to zero.

Statistics Canada. 2012b. "Population growth in Canada: From 1851 to 2061."

So it is that Statistics Canada gurus tell us that the only hope for population increase is immigration. For that to happen, Canada will need to welcome more and more newcomers from other countries over the next few decades. (Figure 2.4)

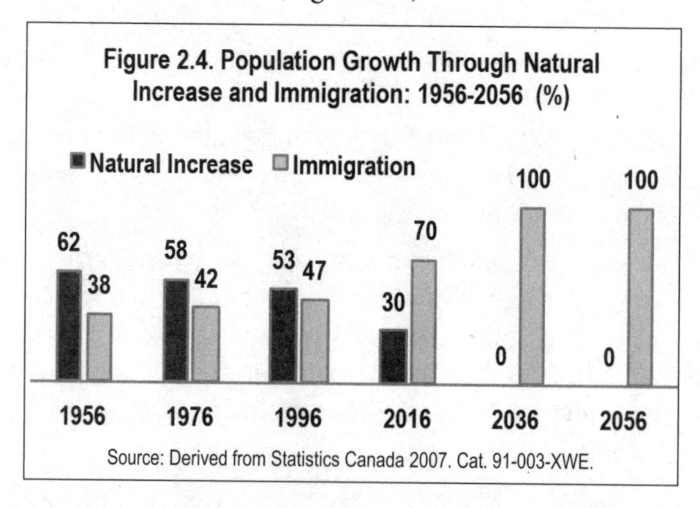

Figure 2.4. Population Growth Through Natural Increase and Immigration: 1956-2056 (%)

Source: Derived from Statistics Canada 2007. Cat. 91-003-XWE.

One major change from the past is the countries of origins of people coming to Canada. As late as the early 1990s, more than half of the new arrivals were still coming from Europe. But by the beginning of the 21st century, the majority were arriving from elsewhere, led by Asian countries. Statistics Canada projects that by 2021, more than 50% of immigrants will come from Asia – a pattern that will continue into the foreseeable future.

The implications for religious groups is dramatic. Groups that used to rely primarily on Europe for many of their new members have seen that pipeline reduced to a relative trickle of people. In contrast, groups like Catholics, Muslims and evangelicals are experiencing a tremendous influx of people. The "No Religion" category is also growing via immigration – at this point, from arrivals from China in particular. (Figure 2.5)

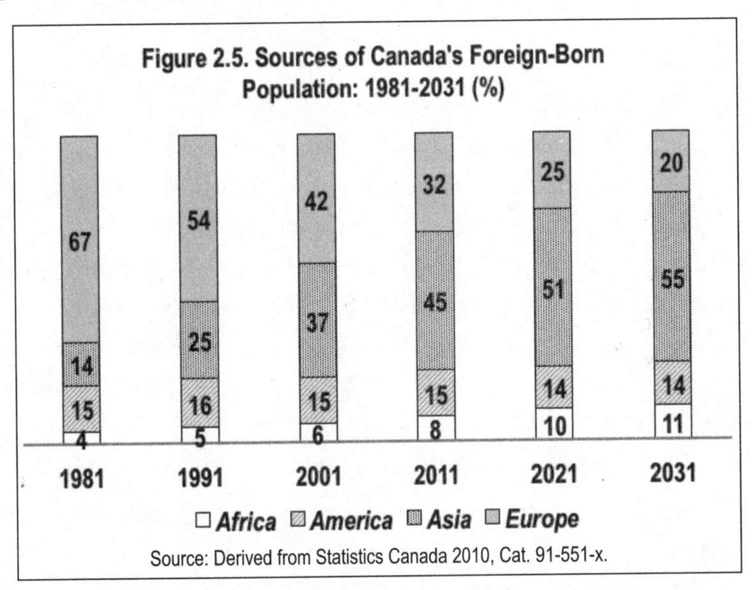

A common belief is that immigration is contributing an ever-diversifying religious mosaic. That's partly true. Groups like Muslims, Hindus, Sikhs and Buddhists have known significant growth since approximately 1990.

But a closer look at the religions people bring to Canada shows that Christian groups, led by Catholics, evangelicals with whom many "generic" Christian immigrants feel affinity, and the Christian Orthodox churches are also benefiting greatly from recent immigration patterns. Between 2000 and 2011, for example, 39% of the people who came to Canada arrived as Muslims, Hindus, Sikhs and Buddhists. However, 44% arrived as either Protestants (23%) or Catholics (21%). The remainder (17%) had no religious affiliation.[6] (Table 2.3)

Table 2.3. Global Distribution of Catholics: 1910 and 2010

	1910	2010
Latin America	24%, 70.7 million	39%, 425.5 million
Europe	65%, 189.0 million	24%, 257.2 million
Sub-Saharan Africa	<1%, 1.2 million	16%, 171.5 million
Asia-Pacific	5%, 13.9 million	12%, 130.5 million
North America	5%, 15.2 million	8%, 88.6 million
Middle East–North Africa	<1%, 1.4 million	<1%, 5.6 million

Source: Pew Research Center, February 13, 2013.

Immigration, by the way, is contributing to greater Catholic diversity in the United States as well. Growing numbers of people are arriving from Mexico and predominantly Catholic countries in Asia, as well as African and Afro-Caribbean countries such as Haiti, Nigeria and Ethiopia.[7] As of 2013, the number of immigrants from Mexico alone numbered close to 13 million people (one third of the population of Canada). The result is that about one-half of U.S. Catholics born since 1980 are Hispanic.[8] Another 2 million immigrants have come from both China and the Philippines, with a further 1.5 million coming from Puerto Rico and the same number from Vietnam.[9]

One key characteristic of Canada's current immigrants is that they tend to be more religiously committed than Canadians who were born in this country. For example, in 2005, 32% of the people living in Canada who were born here attended religious services once a month or more. The figure for people born outside of Canada was 57%. For adults 18 to 34 years old who were born in Canada, the weekly-plus level was also 32%, compared to 53% for those born elsewhere.[10]

This latter pattern could change, depending on the countries of origin of newcomers to Canada. Currently, the leading countries of origin include the Philippines and Pakistan – sources of large numbers of devout Catholics and Muslims respectively.[11] But these days, people coming from such places are adding a new level of fervour to their respective religious groups.

By way of example, Terence Fay notes that since around 1970, "Asian Catholics have been a boon to the Canadian Catholic Church." In addition to establishing vibrant Asian parishes, many have become lay leaders and priests. Between 1990 and 2009, 25% of the men ordained in the Archdiocese of Toronto alone were Asians.[12] As Asian, African and South American seminarians bolster the number of Canadian clergy, says Fay, the result is a more diverse and outward-looking church. They "will help us to shed our parochialism to become truly the international church we profess to be."[13]

Now-retired Archbishop James Weisgerber told a Winnipeg newspaper in 2012 that Filipino immigration, for example, "has been an enormous benefit to the Archdiocese of Winnipeg. We have received thousands of families over the last 40 years and more. They are a vital part of the church community." He points out that Filipinos who have become involved in ethnic parishes have typically contributed to rejuvenated parishes.[14]

Signs of the Times: Immigration Growth in Toronto

The Archdiocese of Toronto is building one brand new church per year to keep from bursting at the seams. "We have opened what we call a mega-church, a large 1,000-person church, once a year for the last 14 years," said Cardinal Thomas Collins of Toronto. Three more are on the drawing board. "The Archdiocese of Toronto is certainly very much influenced by tremendous immigration from all around the world," he said. Mass is celebrated in 37 languages every Sunday in its 225 parishes.

Communications director Neil MacCarthy said that, since 1980, the Archdiocese has been building, on average, a little more than a church each year. Most newcomers have recently been arriving from China, Korea, Vietnam, the Philippines, Sri Lanka, and India. →

"We often refer to the Archdiocese of Toronto as the United Nations of our faith." Many new arrivals, he notes, bring a strong awareness of faith with them. "People come early and stay late."

Cardinal Collins welcomes the immigrants, saying the diversity means "we have a richness in this diocese." However, building and staffing a new church each year is not easy. Many parishes are hiring lay pastoral associates to help out with the work while facing the challenge of bringing in priests and nuns who can speak languages other than English and French.

Agnieszka Krawczynski, *The B.C. Catholic*, May 17, 2015.

Premature Eulogies

John Allen Jr., the highly respected Catholic journalist and Catholic trends analyst, has written that "Even the most committed agnostic or atheist would have to admit that confident predictions made not so long ago about the inevitable decline of religion have proven stunningly false." He points out that, on the contrary, "the late twentieth and early twenty-first century have witnessed a powerful resurgence of religion as a driving force in human affairs."[15] With respect to Catholic numbers globally, Allen puts things this way: "Anybody who thinks this is an era of Catholic decline needs to get out more often."[16]

In Canada, the widespread eulogies for organized religion in Canada in the late 20th century have turned out to be premature and, in all likelihood, will never be warranted. The facts point to a few important realities, led by three that we have underlined.

First, Canadians have not abandoned organized religion. In the Catholic instance, the inclination to see oneself as a Catholic – regardless of one's level of involvement in the Church – remains solidly in place.

Second, a significant development has been the tendency for people who do not value religion to say so. Individuals openly acknowledge that they are not religious; some are very vocal about their atheism. That said, many such people have been getting a lot of ink, leading to an exaggeration of the magnitude of such leanings. It seems clear that what we are seeing is not so much the rejection of religion as the emergence of an explicit kind of polarization. A solid core of people value faith and a solid core do not – with a significant number of Canadians somewhere in between.

Third, in trying to make sense of the religious situation in Canada, including the health and immediate future of our various groups, we often have done so in a geographical vacuum. Our internal gaze has led us to think of evangelism and retention, who we are gaining through birth and who we are losing through death. To return to where the chapter began, we often, as practitioners and researchers, have underemphasized the factor that was responsible for our origins and has been our lifeblood ever since – immigration.

Table 2.4. Immigrant Totals: 2001–2011

	In 1000s	Median Age
Roman Catholic	478	43
No Religion	442	33
Muslim	388	29
Christian*	162	32
Hindu	154	34
Christian Orthodox	108	42
Sikh	107	33
Buddhist	62	38
Pentecostal	41	36
Anglican	23	51
Jewish	21	45
Presbyterian	17	48
United Church	10	52
Lutheran	7	46

*Not included elsewhere.

Source: Statistics Canada.

Immigration is the single most important factor that will determine the future of the Catholic Church in Canada and, for that matter, the future of pretty much everyone and everything else.

That will become readily evident in the research findings that follow.

3

A Closer Look at the Importance and Nature of Faith

Having looked briefly at Catholic origins, historical developments, the rise and alleged fall of the Church in Canada, and signs of new life, we now want to engage today's Catholics in getting a clear reading of where things are at this point in time.

It will be invaluable to hear their thoughts about faith, to learn about their beliefs and to understand their relationship to the Church and parishes. We also want to discuss the "so what?" question with them, which is the extent to which faith is touching their everyday lives – its impact on how they live life and how they deal with death.

The two of us have been speaking with Catholics for some time through our respective national surveys dating back to the 1970s and '80s. But in March 2015, we were able to have an extended conversation about faith with over 3,000 Canadians, including more than 1,000 people raised as Catholics. The result is rich, up-to-date information on religion in Canada generally, and the nature and role of faith in the lives of Catholics specifically.

Our report on our conversations begins with some broad-stroke findings on the importance and nature of faith in the lives of Catholics across the country. Along the way, we will keep an eye on possible changes over time, as well as possible variations by characteristics such as gender and birthplace. It also will be important to explore possible differences when it comes to regional variations, including – obviously – Quebec and the rest of the country.

The Pervasiveness of Catholicism

According to Statistics Canada, almost 13 million Canadians see themselves as Roman Catholics and more than half a million more as Christian Orthodox.

Catholics Are No. 1

As we saw in chapter 1, Catholics were outnumbered by Protestants through 1961. Today, it's no contest. Catholics comprise about 40% of the Canadian population, making them easily the largest religious group in the country. (Table 3.1)

Table 3.1. Religious Groups: 2011
In 1000s

Roman Catholic	12,811	39%
United	2,008	6
Anglican	1,632	5
Christian (generic)	1,476	4
Muslim	1,054	3
Baptist	636	2
Christian Orthodox	551	2
Hindu	498	2
Pentecostal	479	2
Lutheran	478	2
Presbyterian	472	2
Other Christian	1,561	4
Sikh	455	1
Buddhist	367	1
Jewish	329	1
Aboriginal Spirit.	65	<1
No Religion	7,851	24

Source: 2011 National Household Survey.

Protestant groups make up just over 25% of the population, and Other Major Faiths close to 10%. The balance of the population – almost 25% – indicate that they have no religion.

Catholics are also the largest single group in every province and territory except for Nunavut (where their numbers are second to Anglicans). They continue to comprise an overwhelming majority in Quebec and make up close to half of the populations of New Brunswick and Prince Edward Island. Their share of the population is lowest in British Columbia – yet the west coast province is home to the fourth-largest number of Catholics. (Table 3.2)

Table 3.2. Catholics by Province: 2011

In 1000s and % of Province

Quebec	5,776	75%
Ontario	3,977	31
Alberta	866	24
British Columbia	650	15
New Brunswick	366	50
Manitoba	309	26
Nova Scotia	298	33
Saskatchewan	298	30
Newfound/Labrador	182	36
PE Island	59	43
Territories	30	28

Source: 2011 National Household Survey.

The 2015 ARI National Religion Survey

The Angus Reid Institute and Reginald Bibby partnered in carrying out a major new online national survey in March 2015 with a sample of 3,041 Canadians. The survey looked at a wide range of issues, with the questionnaire designed to (a) track responses on some key items over time, (b) provide information on new developments, and (c) examine the merits of the secularization and polarization perspectives. A further objective was to provide comprehensive data on Canada's Catholics.

The sample included 1,152 people who described themselves as Catholics. Further, 1,340 said that their mothers were Catholic and 1,217 reported the same for their fathers. A total of 782 indicated that they had a Catholic spouse or partner. Full methodological details are available at the ARI website (www.angusreid.org/faith-in-canada).

For all the talk about the secularization of Quebec, no less than 75% of the people residing there say they are Catholic. Some 12% indicate they have no religion. The remaining 13% identify with other Christian groups (9%, with 2% Christian Orthodox) and Other World Faiths (4%; 3% Muslim).

In short, there are a lot of Catholics in Canada. Without question, the Catholic Church is the country's biggest religion player, with Protestants – collectively and individually – now running a distant second.

Consequently, to a large extent, as Catholicism goes in Canada, so goes religion as a whole in the country. Those who think religion is in trouble because of the problems of Mainline Protestants have been focusing on the wrong actors. Catholics hold centre stage. (Table 3.3)

Table 3.3. Intergenerational Patterns: Catholics

Catholics with Catholic Mothers

Respondent Catholic	N	Mother Catholic Yes	No	Totals
ALL	**1152**	**95%**	**5**	**100**
Outside Quebec	612	92	8	100
Quebec	539	97	3	100

Source: ARI 2015 Religion Survey.

Indicative of the reality that "Catholics grow their own" is the finding that 95% have come from Catholic homes, as measured by their mothers' religion. The figure is slightly higher in Quebec than elsewhere.

Catholics Stick Like Glue

It is one thing to ask about the religious background of current Catholics. It is another thing to ask, "Given a person was raised in a Catholic home, to what extent does she or he remain a Catholic as an adult?"

The 2015 survey provides us with some decisive information. It shows that Catholics exhibit a remarkable ability to hold on to their people. Some 80% of Canadians who were raised in Catholic homes say that they themselves are Catholics.

Canadian Catholic Survey Bytes
Mother and Respondent Catholic by Age and Gender

18–34	78%	**Women**	84%
35–54	81%	**Men**	79%
55+	84%		

It is widely assumed that intergenerational defection has been particularly high in Quebec since approximately the 1960s, when attendance began to plummet. The common impression is that large numbers of Quebeckers have been abandoning the Catholic faith for "no religion" or secular religious expressions. (Table 3.4)

Table 3.4. Intergenerational Retention: Catholics
Catholic Identity of Those with Catholic Mothers

Mother Catholic	N	*Respondent Catholic* Yes	No	Totals
ALL	**1341**	**81%**	**19**	**100**
Outside Quebec	739	77	24	100
Quebec	600	88	12	100

Source: ARI 2015 Religion Survey.

That's not the case. A somewhat shocking finding is that the level of intergenerational retention is actually *higher in Quebec* (88%) than elsewhere (76%). Yes, there is a measure of defection between generations. But it is more prevalent in other provinces than in Quebec.

For the record, where are "the defectors" headed? The survey provides some answers.

- In Quebec, the 12% of people who are not identifying with their Catholic parents are opting primarily for No Religion (9%), with most of the remaining 3% turning to other Christian groups.
- In the rest of Canada, the 24% who have left Catholicism behind are led by 15% who have moved into the No Religion category, with most of the other 9% having switched to various Christian groups (Mainline Protestants 5%, evangelicals 1%, others 3%).

The findings to this point suggest that the Catholicism that took root in Quebec way back in the early 16th century remains highly pervasive in the province. Ron Graham has observed that a number of Quebec's prominent federal politicians – including Trudeau, Lalonde, Marchand, Pelletier, Sauvé – fought the power of the Church in the 1950s, but "few of them gave up their deep faith."[1] That seems to have been true of much of the province. Many people may have felt dissatisfaction and even some hostility toward the Catholic Church. But through to today, they continued to see themselves as Catholics. Beyond its "staying power" in Quebec, Catholicism is also the dominant religion in the lives of people right across the country.

Beyond Catholic Identification

"Okay," says the cynic, "so lots of people think they are Catholics. But that doesn't mean that they care all that much about faith."

A reasonable point. The good news is that there's a fairly simple way to address it. Let's ask Catholics. That's precisely what we did in our 2015 ARI Religion Survey.

Polarization Inclinations

In keeping with the position we expressed in chapter 2 – that people worldwide have three basic postures toward faith – we offered this statement to our survey participants: "*Some people say Canadians variously (1) embrace religion, (2) reject religion, or (3) are somewhere in between the two extremes.*" We then asked them, "*Where would you tend to locate yourself?*" (Table 3.5)

Table 3.5. Religious Orientations of Catholics and Others

	N	Embrace	Ambivalent	Reject	Totals
All Catholics	**1152**	**35%**	**51%**	**14%**	**100%**
Outside Quebec	612	42	48	10	100
Quebec	540	27	54	19	100
Other Canadians	**1889**	**27**	**40**	**33**	**100**

Source: ARI 2015 Religion Survey.

More than 3 in 10 Catholics say that they are embracing faith, and less than 2 in 10 indicate they are rejecting it. The remaining 5 in 10 are somewhere in the middle. The "embracing" and "ambivalent" levels for Catholics are slightly higher than those of Canadians as a whole.

- The survey shows that Catholics outside Quebec are somewhat more likely than those in Quebec to report that they embrace faith, and slightly less likely to be rejecting it.
- That said, the vast majority of Catholics in Quebec (81%) are not rejecting faith, even if they are somewhat more inclined to say they are ambivalent.

It's interesting and potentially important to note that while about 2 in 10 Quebec Catholics and 1 in 10 Catholics elsewhere say that they are rejecting faith, they nonetheless continue to see themselves as "Catholic."

As emphasized earlier, these kinds of variations – in this case for Catholics – point not to secularization but to polarization. Some people continue to value religion, a small number do not, and many make up an ambivalent middle. Such postures toward religion characterize people everywhere on the planet.

Involvement

The extent to which Catholicism remains entrenched in Quebec and the rest of Canada will come as something of a puzzling finding to many observers. The primary reason is the seemingly self-evident assumption that individuals who value a religion such as Catholicism will be actively involved with a group. On that score, Catholics – especially in Quebec – are not exactly batting 1000.

Our survey shows that about 1 in 4 Catholics (24%) are attending services monthly or more. Outside Quebec the figure is 32%, double the 16% level for Quebec. Monthly-plus attendance is considerably higher for Catholics who embrace faith – 40% in Quebec and 60% elsewhere. (Table 3.6)

Table 3.6. Catholic Attendance Levels* (%)

	Weekly	Monthly	Yearly*	Never	Totals
CATHOLICS	**15**	**9**	**56**	**20**	**100**
Outside Quebec	***22***	***10***	***51***	***17***	***100***
Embrace	44	16	34	6	100
Ambivalent	7	6	67	20	100
Reject	2	3	41	54	100
Quebec	***8***	***8***	***62***	***22***	***100***
Embrace	24	16	50	10	100
Ambivalent	2	5	71	22	100
Reject	4	3	53	40	100
OTHER CANADIANS	**15**	**6**	**42**	**37**	**100**

*Weekly or more; 1-3 times month; less than once a month, hardly ever; never.

Source: 2015 ARI Religion Survey.

Yet it seems important to note that even a large number of Catholics who maintain they embrace faith acknowledge that they seldom attend services. That said, only about 20% indicate that they "never" attend. They do show up once in a while. Still, *the data tell a blunt and sobering tale: for many Catholics, faith is valued far more than group involvement.*

Catholic Staying Power and Seasonal Power

In Bibby's Project Canada national survey in 2000, Canadians who identified with religious groups were asked, "Are you open to the possibility of switching to another religious tradition?"

In Quebec, 98% of Catholics attending monthly or more said "no"; no surprises there. Among Catholics in the province attending less than monthly through never, the figure was 97%! In the rest of Canada, the comparable numbers were 87% and 86% respectively. There is little reason to believe that much has changed.

What about occasional attendance? We partnered on two Christmas surveys in December of 2014 and 2015, and asked Catholics if they expected to attend "a special Christmas service." More than twice the number of regular, monthly-plus attenders indicated they would be present for a Christmas service – meaning that, outside Quebec, attendance would double from about 30% to 60%. In Quebec, the monthly-plus core of 15% would be sharing Christmas pews with an extra 20% or so.

Belonging without being actively involved seems like a puzzling paradox. Cardinal Thomas Collins writes that "the Sunday Eucharist should be the high point in our week as disciples of Christ, for on that day we celebrate the resurrection of the Lord. Sunday is a time to stop, look, and listen." He continues on to say that "we need to have a break from the daily rush of activity, a time to be with family, to be with God," adding, "In fact, the busier we are, the more we need Sabbath time every day, and certainly at least once a week." He concludes, "There is no substitute for the Holy Eucharist on the Day of the Lord."[2]

Given that Catholic leaders therefore have seemingly instilled a norm of being present for mass at least once a week, how can "a good Catholic" claim to be embracing faith when they are not attending services regularly? Wouldn't people at least feel some guilt over only showing up a few times a year? (Table 3.7)

Table 3.7. Catholic Views of Service Attendance

	CATHOLICS			OTHER
	All (1151)	Outside QC (612)	Quebec (539)	CANS (1889)
My parents felt that they were "supposed to go to church"	66%	65	67	52
In my mind, people who attend religious services should not go because they feel they have to but because they find it to be worthwhile	72	75	70	79
I prefer to live life without God or congregation: *Disagree*	71	75	67	58
I sometimes feel guilty for not being more involved in religion	35	48	20	31

Source: ARI 2015 Religion Survey.

Well, actually, about 1 in 2 Catholics outside Quebec *do* say they feel guilty for not being more involved, as do some 1 in 3 other Canadians. But, in the case of Quebec, skipping mass is only creating guilt pangs among 1 in 5 Catholics. (Figure 3.1)

What seems to trouble academics – not to mention Catholic leaders – does not seem to trouble a fairly large number of Catholics.

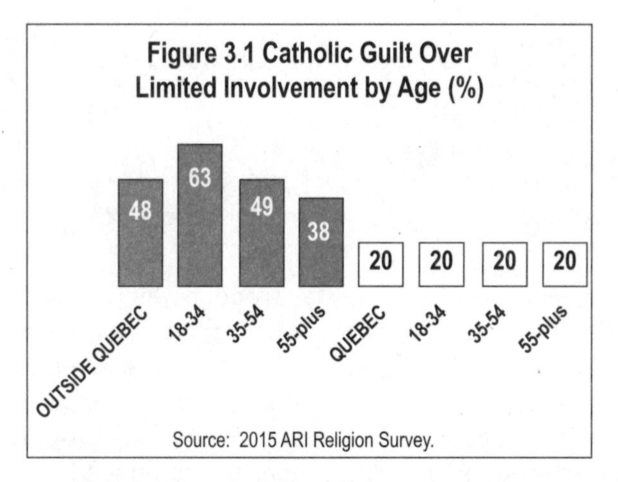

In short, significant numbers of Catholics, particularly in Quebec, continue to identify with the faith and to value it. Yet they don't feel the need to be active attenders.

But hold on a moment: that's not to say that inactive Catholics want nothing from the Church or that the Catholic faith doesn't matter to them. Remember that some 80% are attending services at least once in a while. In addition, over half report that they have attended a religious funeral in the past year and about one quarter have attended a religious wedding. And some 6 in 10 say that when they die, they want to have a religious funeral. A majority of Catholics also feel that it is important for parents to teach their children religious beliefs, presumably with some input from parishes. (Table 3.8)

Table 3.8. Rites of Passage and Views of Religious Beliefs and the Church

	CATHOLICS			OTHER
	All (1152)	Outside QC (612)	Quebec (539)	CANS (1889)
Have attended a religious wedding in the past year	24%	31	16	24
Have attended a religious funeral in the past year	56	56	56	39
When you die, want to have a religious funeral	57	56	58	31
It's important for parents to teach their children religious beliefs	71	80	61	55
I have a high level of confidence in religious leaders	35	41	27	25
Pope Francis is having a positive impact on the world	84	92	76	69

Source: ARI 2015 Religion Survey.

The Persistence of Catholics' Catholicism: The American Example

How American Catholics construe what it means to be Catholic is remarkably resilient. It is evident from our series of surveys that Catholics today, as they have done for at least 25 years, define Catholicism on their own terms.

Some readers and observers may wonder why Catholics bother being Catholic or calling themselves Catholic if their Catholicism is so apparently diffuse and selectively independent of church teachings and church authority. But Catholicism is far more internally differentiated and encrusted by pluralistic strands than is often acknowledged. Church leaders and commentators are free to shake their heads at what may often seem to be a lazy Catholicism. [But] it does a disservice to the theology and sociology of Catholicism to try to package it, or to expect it to be packaged into some monolithic, undifferentiated, and uncomplicated thing.

William D'Antonio, Michele Dillon, and Mary Gautier. *American Catholics in Transition*, 2013:K2481, 2488, 2494, 2507, 2533, 2539.

When it comes to religious leadership, Catholics are not particularly generous with their endorsements. Just 3 in 10 indicate that they have a high level of confidence in religious leaders generally – 41% outside Quebec and only 27% in Quebec.

That all changes for most Catholics when it comes to Pope Francis. A resounding 84% feel he is having a positive impact on the world – 76% in Quebec, and no less than 92% elsewhere. Among young adults under 35, the respective endorsement figures are 68% in Quebec, 85% in the rest of the country.

Views of Pope Francis... *one year in*

	Practising	Non-Practising
Overall positive: Pope Francis	90%	66
Overall positive: RC Church	**91**	**71**
Positive: Less focus on sexuality	70	72
Positive: Living less luxurious life	**93**	**85**
More emphasis on helping the poor	95	84
Has not done enough on sexual abuse	**32**	**40**
Overall: improved opinion RC Church	63	39
Has had impact on you revisiting your tie with the RC Church	***	**14**

An ARI survey in March of 2014 compared the views of Pope Francis held by self-described "practising" and "non-practising" Catholics. Solid majorities in both categories gave the Pope a positive general assessment. They particularly applauded him for putting less focus on sexuality and emphasizing living a simpler, less luxurious life, as well as the need to help poor people.

Overall, 71% of non-practising Catholics gave the Roman Catholic Church a positive rating – only slightly below the 91% level of practising Catholics. However, asked if Pope Francis has had an impact on their revisiting their ties with the Church, only 14% of the inactive indicated "yes." But perhaps that's a modest start.

Belief

Major components of religious commitment, according to well-worn thinking in the social sciences dating back to Charles Glock and Rodney Stark,[3] are belief, practice, experience and knowledge. The two pioneering researchers at the University of California at Berkeley argued that all religions feature these four "dimensions." Their basic summation continues to be a highly accurate lens for determining how religious individuals – including Catholics – are.

Survey participants were asked about a large number of beliefs, some fairly conventional, others a bit less standard. What is readily apparent is that Catholics and other Canadians do not lack for supernatural beliefs at this point in Canadian history.

Beliefs about God, heaven, life after death, the divinity of Jesus, and angels are held by a majority of people, led in many instances by Catholics. Even the idea of hell is endorsed by close to half the

population. Belief levels are consistently higher outside Quebec – but only slightly, in most instances. (Table 3.9)

Table 3.9. Select Less Conventional Beliefs
"Do you believe..."
% Indicating "Yes, I definitely believe" or "Yes, I think so"

	CATHOLICS All (1151)	Outside QC (612)	Quebec (539)	OTHER CANS (1889)
Miraculous healing sometimes occurs	75	77	74	64
Some people have psychic powers enabling them to predict events	57	57	57	48
We can have contact with the spirit world	55	53	59	47
You yourself have experienced an event before it happened (precognition)	53	50	57	46
That we can communicate with the dead	53	49	58	36
In astrology	39	40	38	33
That you yourself will be reincarnated	39	34	44	29

Source: ARI 2015 Religion Survey.

Catholics outdistance the country as a whole in their tendency to hold an array of additional, "less conventional" supernatural-related beliefs. In this case, belief levels tend to be similar for Catholics in Quebec and elsewhere. (Table 3.10)

Table 3.10. Select Conventional Beliefs
"Do you believe..."
% Indicating "Yes, I definitely believe" or "Yes, I think so"

	CATHOLICS All (1151)	Outside QC (612)	Quebec (539)	OTHER CANS (1889)
That God or a higher power exists	83	86	80	67
In heaven	76	81	69	56
In life after death	73	74	72	61
That Jesus was the Divine Son of God	73	75	70	51
God/higher power cares about you personally	72	73	72	54
You yourself have spiritual needs	72	74	70	64
In angels	70	73	68	57
In hell	47	56	37	39

Source: ARI 2015 Religion Survey.

We are talking here about things like belief in miraculous healing, people having psychic powers, one's own experience of precognition, being able to have contact with the spirit world, and – more specifically – being able to communicate with the dead. All of these kinds of beliefs are held by more than 5 in 10 Catholics.

In addition, some 4 in 10 of Canada's Catholics also express belief in astrology. A similar proportion maintain that they themselves will be reincarnated. Neither of these ideas, of course, is endorsed by mainline Catholic theology. The reincarnation level (39%) is quite a bit higher than that recently uncovered for American Catholics (28%). Nonetheless, as one American professor has playfully put things, "Most Catholics who believe in reincarnation for one reason or another just go on being Catholic. They are no more troubled by their departure from Church guidance on the subject than on birth control."[4] Esteemed Canadian philosopher Charles Taylor puts things this way: "More and more people adopt what would earlier have been seen as untenable positions, e.g., they consider themselves Catholic while not accepting many crucial dogmas, or they combine Christianity with Buddhism, or they pray while not being certain they believe." Taylor adds, "This is not to say that people didn't occupy positions like this in the past. Just that now it seems to be easier to be upfront about it."[5]

Here, as with attendance patterns, we see evidence of Catholic autonomy. People continue to view themselves as Catholic and value the faith. At the same time, when it comes to attendance and beliefs, they exhibit a pronounced tendency to be into what I and others have described now for some time as "religion à la carte."

These patterns are remarkably similar to what William D'Antonio and his associates have been finding in examining the beliefs, attitudes and values of American Catholics in their five national surveys spanning the late 1980s through today. By the early 1990s, they noted the ongoing importance across gender and generations of beliefs relating to Jesus, the sacraments, Mary as the Mother of God, and concern for the poor. But there was a trend away from regular mass attendance and obedience to traditional teachings in favour of

conscience.[6] For many, "being a good Catholic" has become "largely independent of the church hierarchy's teachings."[7]

Such à la carte tendencies are further readily evident when we look at personal religious practices.

Practice

Religions typically call for their adherents to engage not only in public practices but in private practices as well. In the case of Catholicism, the devout have been expected to pray privately, perhaps give thanks for food, and – to some extent – include Bible reading as part of their personal devotions or spiritual meditations.

These days, one might supplement such private religious activities by drawing on technology – making use of television, maybe the Internet, maybe something else, including reading Catholic newsletters and newspapers.[8]

In our survey, we asked Catholics and others about the extent to which they engage in an illustrative number of activities. Weekly service attendance is included at the top of the list for the purpose of comparing public and private practices. (Table 3.11)

Table 3.11. Practices

"How often do you..."

% Indicating Weekly or More"

	CATHOLICS			OTHER
	All	Outside QC	Quebec	CANS
	(1151)	(612)	(539)	(1889)
Attend religious services	15%	22	8	16
Pray privately/individually	41	45	37	36
Read your horoscope	19	21	18	15
Say table grace/give thanks for food	15	21	7	21
Discuss your faith with family or friends	10	13	7	18
Read the Bible, Quran, or other sacred text	8	12	5	17
Watch religious TV programs	6	5	8	6
Practise other spiritual activities online	5	7	4	6
Discuss something about faith online	4	4	3	7
Watch worship services online	3	5	1	5

Source: ARI 2015 Religion Survey.

Salt + Light Television and the Salt and Light Catholic Media Foundation

Salt + Light Television and the Salt and Light Catholic Media Foundation were founded on the wings of World Youth Day 2002 in Toronto by the highly successful communications entrepreneur Gaetano Gagliano, who realized his dream of establishing a Catholic Communications Platform for Canada and for the world. He had one desire: to communicate the message of the Gospel and the story of the Church with joy and hope. The Gagliano family entrusted the realization of their dream to Basilian Father Thomas Rosica, who had headed up the highly successful World Youth Day 2002 in Toronto.

S|L
SALT AND LIGHT
Catholic Media Foundation

Salt and Light is more than a TV network that broadcasts 24/7 in Canada. It is a multi-platform communications enterprise serving the world through TV, radio, Internet and print, with a high class magazine. In addition to nearly 3 million subscribers in Canada, Salt and Light broadcasts its message in English, French, Italian, Cantonese and Mandarin, with more languages on the way.

After 13 years of existence, Salt and Light reaches millions around the world through its live streaming and on-demand features. The goal of Salt and Light: to bring the flavour of the Gospel and the light of Christ to the world. Its most unique feature: the principal protagonists and actors are young adults who carry on the legacy of World Youth Day 2002 in Canada.

Source: Salt + Light website: www.saltandlighttv.org.

What is readily apparent is that the leading private practice activity is prayer. Some 40% of Catholics say that they pray privately at least once a week – 45% outside Quebec, 37% in Quebec. That level readily exceeds service attendance. (Figure 3.2)

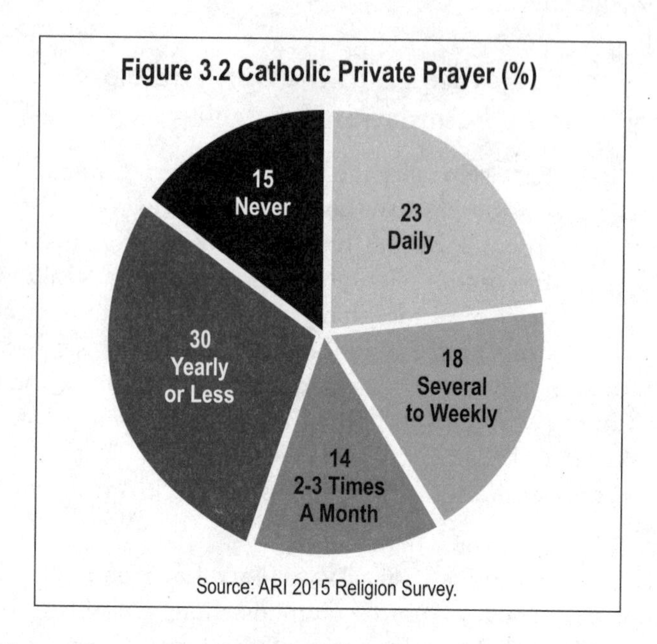

Figure 3.2 Catholic Private Prayer (%)

Source: ARI 2015 Religion Survey.

Table grace – among religious practices – comes in a fairly distant second at 15%, and is quite a bit more common in so-called English Canada. Coincidentally, it matches Catholic attendance levels.

About 1 in 10 Catholics – led by those outside Quebec – indicate that social support for faith involving family and friends is a common activity for them. Some 8% are weekly Bible readers, but they are readily outnumbered by horoscope readers (19%). Other devotional and worship activities involving TV and the Internet are practised by fairly small numbers.

Experience

Christianity is among the religions that gives considerable emphasis to the importance of experience. God is not simply a concept that is the object of belief. For Christians, God is a Being who relates to people and is related to as a living reality. At the heart of Christian faith – and Catholic faith – is the idea that one has a relationship with God, which reflects itself in the conviction that one is experiencing God.

Our latest survey has found that more than 1 in 2 Catholics across the country believe that they have experienced God's presence. But this, for large numbers, is not a one-time thing. About 1 in 4 Catholics say that they experience God's presence on a weekly to daily basis. Make it monthly and the figure increases further to 1 in 3.

For Catholics and many other Canadians, the experience of the supernatural does not stop with God.

We saw earlier that some 70% of Catholics and close to 60% of other Canadians believe in the existence of angels. Well, that's not all: virtually the same proportion of Catholics and 50% of others further believe that they have been protected by a guardian angel. (Table 3.12)

Table 3.12. Experience

"Do you believe..."

% Indicating "Yes, I definitely believe" or "Yes, I think so"

	CATHOLICS			OTHER
	All (1151)	Outside QC (612)	Quebec (539)	CANS (1889)
You have experienced God's presence	54	54	55	43
Experience God's presence weekly or more	26	29	22	24
You have been protected by a guardian angel	68	65	70	50

Source: ARI 2015 Religion Survey.

More than a few people may be wondering, Is that something that older generations of Catholics bought into? The answer is "Not really." It's true that the belief is a bit more prevalent among people 55 and over, but not by very much. Those slight differences by age cohort mean little – if we all keep in mind that people in the latter two younger age cohorts still have a lot of years to be protected by guardian angels!

Canadian Catholic Survey Bytes

Believe they have been protected from harm by a guardian angel: age and gender

18–34	64%	**Women**	75%
35–54	67%	**Men**	59%
55+	70%		

Knowledge

A fourth "dimension" of religious commitment is knowledge. The assumption here is that people who claim to be devout would be expected to know some of the basic content of their religious traditions.

A devout Catholic, for example, would surely know the name of the individual who "denied Jesus three times." Another prosaic bit of information she or he should be able to offer to an inquisitive outsider is the name of the first book in the Old Testament.

Now let's be clear. We could get theologically sophisticated: one of us has a theology degree and the other has been immersed in Catholic thought for much of his life. But our point is that these two simple questions – while anything but a test of Catholic knowledge – should be questions that a devout Catholic can answer correctly without thinking twice.

So we put the two questions to Catholics and other Canadians in our 2015 survey.

- What we found is that only about 1 in 4 non-Catholics knew the person who denied Jesus three times. But almost 1 in 2 could identify Genesis as the first book in the Old Testament. Some 24% were able to answer both questions correctly. (Figure 3.3)

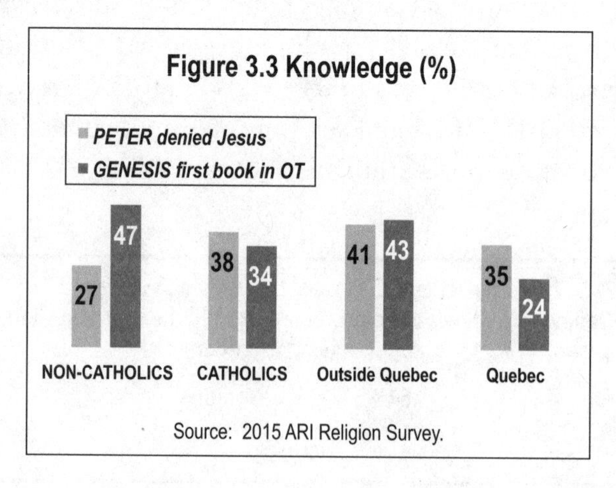

- And as for Catholics? Well, they fared better than non-Catholics in identifying Peter as the denier of Jesus (38% vs. 27%). However, they got walloped on the Genesis question (47% for non-Catholics vs. their 34%). The Catholic figure for answering both queries correctly: 22% nationally, with Quebec coming in at 15% and the rest of the country at 29%. Had the number of knowledge questions been expanded, there is little reason to believe things would be much brighter. A 2008 poll conducted for Radio-Canada, for example, showed that only 11% of Quebeckers could name the four Evangelists.[9]

Again, we emphasize that these are two very simple measures of Christian knowledge. Nonetheless, the results suggest that large numbers of Canada's Catholics today are not well informed about some of the basics of their faith.

These findings do raise a significant question: in light of low attendance levels and low levels of personal study, as suggested by extremely low levels of Bible reading, it is not at all clear how average Catholics are sustaining an awareness of the basics of faith, even if many of them attended Catholic schools when they were growing up. As Thomas Groome notes, these days people have become proactive in seeking out what they need. "Walk along the aisles of a Home Depot and you'll find hundreds of do-it-yourself carpenters, plumbers, and painters. Surely this should be true in matters of faith as well," he says. "All it takes is a bit of effort; the resources are readily available."[10]

The need for ongoing Catholic education – for catechesis – seems apparent.

And things have been getting worse...

Research over the years shows Canadians – and Catholics – to be becoming increasingly inept when it comes to very basic religious questions. In 1975, 52% of people across the country could identify Peter as the denier of Jesus, including 63% of Catholics. By 2000, the figure had slipped to 42% nationally and to 47% for Catholics. Today, 31% of Canadians know the answer to the question, including, as noted above, 38% of Catholics. As for identifying Genesis as the first book in the Old Testament, 59% of Canadians could do so in 1995 versus 42% today. The Catholic level then: 58%; now the above 34%.

The information age allows us to know a great deal about pretty much everything. However, it seems clear that fewer Canadians are bothering to learn very much about the basics of Judeo-Christianity.

The Consequential Dimension

In their original identification of key dimensions of religious commitment, Glock and Stark included a fifth dimension: "the consequential dimension." They pointed out that all major religious traditions maintain that faith is more than about belief, practice, experience and knowledge.

The expectation is that religious commitment will lead to personal and collective results. They eventually concluded that, rather than being conceptualized as a fifth component of commitment, it was more accurate and more helpful to see to what extent people who claim to be religiously committed are influenced by the faiths they value.

Having looked at identification, the embracing of faith, and a number of dimensions of religious commitment, we now want to turn our attention to what people who profess Catholic faith – as well as many observers of Catholicism – regard as the critically important question: the impact that faith is having on life and lives.

4

A Closer Look at the Impact of Faith on Life

Christian faith has much to say about personal and social well-being. People's relationship with God is expected to have an impact on those who embrace faith and, in turn, on how they relate to others. Christian faith also has much to say about death, placing our individual lives and historical periods into nothing less than an eternal context.

As a result, faith should be having an impact on Canada's Catholics. Here's what we found.

The Extent to Which Faith is Enriching Life

Faith as a Resource

"Whether or not they fully subscribe to the official theology, most Catholics" – says John Allen Jr. – "feel in their bones that the Church is the place where they encounter God, where their hunger for the divine and the transcendent is fed. It's their spiritual home, their family."[1] Consistent with such an observation, about 1 in 4 Catholics across Canada say they feel strengthened by their faith every day through every week. The figure increases to 1 in 2 for those who feel that way at least once a month. (Table 4.1)

Table 4.1. Feel Strengthened by One's Faith
"How often do you..."
% Indicating Weekly or More

	CATHOLICS			OTHER
	ALL	ROC	Quebec	CANS
	(1152)	(612)	(539)	(1889)
Feel strengthened by your faith				
Daily	13	15	10	18
Weekly	13	16	9	13
Monthly	14	15	14	9
Seldom	32	34	30	21
Never	28	20	37	39
Feel strengthened "Daily to Weekly"				
Weekly Attenders	78	76	86	91
Embrace Faith	53	59	43	74

Source: ARI 2015 Religion Survey.

As would be expected, the sentiment of feeling strengthened by faith is considerably higher among weekly attenders than others (78%), both in Quebec (86%) and elsewhere (76%). Among other Canadian weekly attenders, the level is 91%.

More than half of those Catholics who indicate that they "embrace" faith – apart from attendance – also are significantly more likely than others to feel strengthened by faith "daily" to "weekly." The level for other Canadians who embrace faith and find faith to be a resource is even higher: 74%.

We asked Catholics and other Canadians who attend services at least once a month, "*What is the MAIN THING your religious involvement adds to your life?*" Based on extensive previous research,[2] three response options were offered: *God and spirituality*, *personal enrichment*, and *the people*. We also provided the opportunity for people to cite other significant contributions of faith to life.

Here we found noteworthy differences between Catholics in Quebec and elsewhere. (Table 4.2)

Table 4.2. What Involvement Adds to One's Life

"What is the *MAIN THING* your *religious involvement adds to your life?"*

Monthly-Plus Attenders

		CATHOLICS		OTHER
	ALL	ROC	Quebec	CANS
	(279)	(194)	(85)	(408)
God and spirituality	46	54	31	56
Personal enrichment	36	31	47	23
The people	12	8	20	15
Other	6	7	2	6
TOTALS100	100	100	100	

Source: 2015 ARI Religion Survey.

- Outside Quebec, Catholics were most inclined to cite God and spirituality, followed by personal enrichment. In Quebec, the rank order was reversed.
- "The people" received a higher level of endorsement in Quebec (20%) than elsewhere (8%).
- Among other Canadians, personal enrichment is given a bit less play.

The sample numbers are fairly small. But tentatively, at least, the findings suggest that the communal aspect of religious involvement may be somewhat more important among Catholics in Quebec than elsewhere. Conversely, in other provinces as a whole, the worship and Eucharist components of attendance are perhaps more important than the social dimension.

These findings tell us that, overall, large numbers of Catholics and other Canadians believe that faith functions as an important resource to them as they live out life. It variously brings God and spirituality to their lives, and variously contributes to their personal and social needs.

Faith as a Source of Happiness

Catholics and other Canadians differ little with respect to the importance of key sources of happiness. For pretty much everyone, family, relationships and friends are of primary importance.

Differences are minor by service attendance and between Quebec and the rest of the country.

Some observers make the mistake of assuming that "no difference means no influence." That's not true.

What the lack of variation shows is that people who value faith and those who do not are just as likely to receive enjoyment from these various parts of their lives. Faith may be a source factor for some, but it isn't for others. People who are not active Catholics or – in the case of other Canadians, active in religious groups – are finding alternative ways of enjoying life. Conversely, people who value faith are no less likely than others to be receiving high levels of enjoyment from these parts of life. (Table 4.3)

Table 4.3. Catholics and Enjoyment of Life

% Indicating Receive "A Great Deal" or "Quite a Bit" of Enjoyment

	CATHOLICS					OTHER CANS
	ALL	ROC		Quebec		
		Monthly+	*Less*	*Monthly+*	*Less*	
	(1152)	(194)	(418)	(86)	(454)	(1889)
Your child/children	92%	96%	90%	90%	92%	92%
Your family life generally	90	93	89	92	89	85
Your marriage/relationship	88	94	85	91	87	88
Your leisure activities	85	88	89	82	79	85
Your friends	82	86	81	91	78	81
Your house or apartment	81	79	79	89	82	73
Your pet(s)	80	75	85	75	80	83
Your job	60	60	52	77	63	55

*Percentaging based on eliminating non-applicable responses.

Source: ARI 2015 Religion Survey.

Put succinctly, faith is not a unique source of personal happiness. But for many, it is an important source.

What about relational and personal happiness? How do Catholics compare with others?

The survey has found that Catholics and other Canadians generally differ little in the relational and personal happiness levels they report.

Contrary to what many think about widespread divorce signalling widespread marital unhappiness, when people are together, they are surprisingly upbeat about their relationships.

Actually, that doesn't surprise either of us. We both have been documenting the same reality in our various surveys dating back to the '70s and '80s.

When it comes to marriage...

		CATHOLICS				OTHER
	ALL	ROC		Quebec		CANS
		Monthly+	Less	Monthly+	Less	
	(8348)	(2262)	(3131)	(570)	(2334)	(13,959)
Married	47	57	50	46	34	52
Never married	18	14	21	12	20	19
Common-law	12	3	9	6	25	6
Widowed	12	17	8	25	8	12
Divorced	8	6	8	8	10	8
Separated	3	3	4	3	3	3

Statistics Canada, General Social Survey, 2012

- Catholics differ little from Canadians as a whole in their inclination to marry or not marry or stay married.
- The exception is less active Catholics in Quebec, who are disproportionately young and less likely to be married and more likely to be in common-law relationships.
- Reflecting age, widowhood is more prevalent among active Catholics, especially in Quebec.
- On September 8, 2015, Pope Francis reaffirmed traditional teachings on the "indissolubility of marriage," but streamlined annulment procedures, saying they needed to be speeded up so that Catholics are not "long oppressed by darkness of doubt" over whether their marriages would be declared null and void. The changes, seen by many as the most significant in centuries, include the need to eliminate a second review of situations by a cleric, giving bishops the option of fast-tracking annulments in certain circumstances, and making the process free of charge beyond nominal administrative fees, and completed in 45 days.

Sources: Thomson Reuters, CBC, CNN

- Some 9 in 10 Catholics who are married or in a relationship say they are either "very happy" or "pretty happy." Active attendees in Quebec are a bit less effusive about their ties, and Catholics there and elsewhere who are not attending very much are somewhat more inclined than others to report unhappy relationships. Overall, however, the Catholic relationship situation is similar to others. (Table 4.4)

Table 4.4. Catholics and Happiness (%)

	CATHOLICS					
	All	ROC		Quebec		OTHER CANS
		Monthly+	*Less*	*Monthly+*	*Less*	
	(1152)	(194)	(418)	(86)	(454)	(1889)
Marriage/Relationship						
Very happy	46	54	47	37	44	45
Pretty happy	44	41	41	60	45	48
Not too happy	10	5	12	3	17	7
Personally						
Very happy	21	25	21	27	18	23
Pretty happy	67	68	64	68	69	65
Not too happy	12	7	15	5	13	12

Source: ARI 2015 Religion Survey.

- As for personal happiness, Catholics and other people are considerably more restrained. About 2 in 10 tell us they are "very happy," and another 7 in 10 indicate they are "pretty happy." There are about the same proportion of unhappy Catholics as other Canadians (1 in 10), but they tend to be somewhat more numerous among those who attend services less than once a month.

- Enjoyment and satisfaction among Catholics differs only mildly by age and gender; people 55 and older are slightly more likely than younger cohorts to report higher levels of enjoyment of family and relationships.

Canadian Catholic Survey Bytes
Enjoyment and Happiness: Age and Gender

	Enjoyment		*Happiness*	
	Family	Friends	Relational	Personal
	"Great Deal" or "Quite a Bit"		"Very/Pretty"	"Very/Pretty"
18–34	86%	84%	44–46%	17–67%
35–54	89	77	41–46	17–68
55+	92	85	52–42	27–66
Women	91	84	46–43	21–66
Men	88	79	47–46	21–68

Faith as a Means of Addressing Life's Big Questions

Previous surveys dating back to the 1970s have found that around 9 in 10 Canadians maintain that they think about life's big, "ultimate questions" at least at some points in their lives.[3] We are thinking here of questions regarding life's purpose, why suffering takes place, how a person can experience happiness, and what happens after death. Charles Taylor has written that, in the midst of widespread secularity, when it comes to the question of what makes human life worth living or what confers meaning, "Most of us are still in the process of groping for answers."[4] (Figure 4.1)

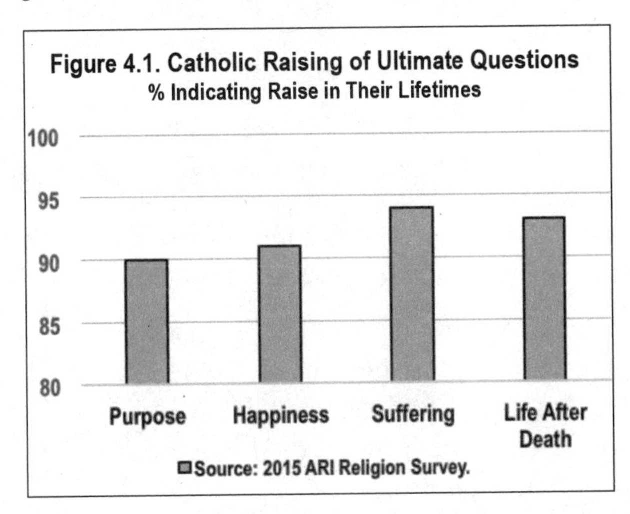

Figure 4.1. Catholic Raising of Ultimate Questions
% Indicating Raise in Their Lifetimes

Canada's Catholics today are no exception. What's interesting to see is the extent to which they feel they have found answers to these "big questions."

We have already seen that close to 75% believe in life after death, with close to the same proportion believing in heaven and about 50% in hell. When it comes to life's purpose, Catholics and others are not quite so sure.

- Only about one third – led by those in Quebec – feel at least quite certain that they have found the answer to the meaning of life, while another third admit they are "rather uncertain." The remaining third say they don't think there's an answer to the question. (Table 4.5)

Table 4.5. Certainty About the Meaning of Life

"How sure are you that you have found the answer to the meaning of life?" (%)

	Very Certain	Quite Certain	Rather Uncertain	Is No Answer	Totals
ALL CATHOLICS	**8**	**24**	**32**	**36**	**100**
ROC	8	18	37	37	100
Quebec	7	31	28	34	100
Monthly-Plus	18	35	24	23	100
Less Often	4	21	35	40	100
18–34	9	24	36	31	100
35–54	7	22	34	37	100
55+	7	27	28	38	100
Females	6	22	34	38	100
Males	9	27	31	33	100
OTHER CANS	**15**	**17**	**24**	**44**	**100**

Source: 2015 ARI Religion Survey.

- Other Canadians are slightly more polarized between certainty on the one hand and feeling there is no answer on the other.
- Variations among Catholics are intriguing: monthly-plus attenders (53%) are far more inclined than infrequent attenders (25%) to feel they have resolved the question – although 40% of the latter indicate that they simply don't think there's an answer to the question.

So far these numbers may seem a bit cold and lifeless. We are about to add some life.

An additional survey that we carried out together in March of 2014 allows us to amplify and clarify our current finding of about 75% of Catholics believing in life after death. That survey offers some valuable insights into a variety of ideas that Catholics and other Canadians have concerning this important topic.

For starters, the survey also documented the fact that Canadians as a whole (80%) continue to be reluctant to rule out the possibility that there is life after death. But what we found amazing is the extent to which Canadians embrace a wide range of ideas about the ongoing presence of people who have died.

- Led by active attenders, 6 in 10 Catholics believe that *people who have died are aware of what is happening in our lives*, and 5 in 10 think it *is possible to communicate with those who are gone*. Moreover, 4 in 10 say they *have felt in touch* with someone who has died.
- Active attendance is strongly associated with Catholics believing that they *will one day see people again who have died*, and the expectation that *they themselves will go to heaven* when they die. Those who are active Catholics also are more likely than others to say that their *primary emotional response to death is one of hope*.

The reality of death and the fascination with the question of life after death – including widespread belief that interaction is taking place with "those who have gone before" – represents a vast "market" for the Catholic Church and other religious groups that have something to say.

Why Religion Endures

Many of the secularization faithful ... assume that few people around the world today ever think about the "big" philosophical questions such as the meaning and purpose of life. But, that's not so. The overwhelming majority of people on earth do think about the meaning and purpose of life. Regional variations are modest, ranging from 89 percent in Sub-Saharan Africa to 76 percent in Asia.

What do they conclude? People want to know *why* the universe exists, and they don't want their lives to be pointless. Only religion provides credible and satisfactory answers to the great existential questions. Secularists have been predicting the imminent demise of religion for centuries. They have always been wrong – and their claims today are no different.

Rodney Stark, *The Triumph of Faith*, 2015, K4135, 4162.

Faith as a Resource in Times of Need

As Catholics and others live out life in Canada, everyone – to varying degrees – knows the reality of strain and pain. It is important to have a sense of what kinds of issues trouble Catholics, as well as the potential for faith and parish involvement to have a neutralizing impact, so that it is possible to respond and help to elevate lives.

We posed a list of eight fairly common personal concerns that Canadians have expressed over the years, and asked survey participants to what extent these are currently areas of concern for them.

Three themes topped the list, cited by more than 1 in 2 Catholics and close to the same proportions of other Canadians: *concerns about one's children*, *health* and *lack of money*.

When one thinks about tangible ministry to Catholics in the form of touching their lives at key points of need, these three areas should be among the primary focal points. They tend to be the three top concerns of active and inactive attenders alike – both in Quebec and in the rest of the country.

Almost 1 in 2 Catholics also express concern about the fact that they feel they *should be getting more out of life*. Significantly, levels of concern are higher among infrequent attenders than those who are highly involved in parish life. (Table 4.6)

Table 4.6. Catholics and Personal Concerns

% Indicating Concerned "A Great Deal" or "Quite a Bit"

	CATHOLICS					OTHER CANS
	ALL	ROC		Quebec		
		Monthly+	*Less*	*Monthly+*	*Less*	
	(1152)	(194)	(418)	(86)	(454)	(1889)
Concerns about your children*	58	57	49	67	65	48
Your health	57	45	42	73	74	42
Lack of money	52	46	46	50	62	45
Feeling you should be getting more out of life	48	37	47	46	54	41
Never have enough time	44	40	44	47	46	43
Getting older	39	30	38	43	44	34
Your marriage/relationship*	33	28	23	52	43	22
Loneliness	32	25	26	42	39	26

*Percentaging based on eliminating non-applicable responses.

Source: ARI 2015 Religion Survey.

A fairly uniform concern for just under 1 in 2 Catholics is the sense that they *never seem to have enough time*. Three issues of concern for about 1 in 3 – led by those in Quebec – are *aging*, *relationships* and *loneliness*.

Two general patterns are worth noting. First, differences in concern by service attendance are generally inconsistent and small. Second, concern levels are consistently higher in Quebec than elsewhere – a pattern evident in our surveys probing concerns dating back to the 1970s.

The proverbial bottom line? Personal concerns seemingly are an inevitable part of life. One is reminded of the famous Buddhist saying, something to the effect that "Life is difficult."[5] As we saw earlier, some 1 in 3 Catholics who are involved in parishes across the country say that one of the key things they receive from their participation is personal enrichment. Catholics, as with Canadians generally, have an ongoing need for such responses.

The Extent to Which Faith is Influencing Outlook

Faith and Values

Christian faith stresses many interpersonal values that take something of a goals and means form. For example, the goal for much of everything is summed up in "The Great Commandment" – the classic admonition of Jesus that we love God with all our heart and our neighbour as ourselves.

The means include a number of traits such as honesty, forgiveness, courtesy and generosity. People who are committed to the Christian faith are expected both to place importance on such values and to live them out. Values have both idea and behavioural components.

Our 2015 survey asked Canadians to rate a number of illustrative traits. We found that *family life* was viewed as "very important" by close to 80%, led by people who are active in parishes. Comparatively, *material comfort* and *personal success* were far behind.

Spirituality and *religion* were a distant third among these five goal-like values posed – except for Catholics who are actively involved in parishes, for whom these two values are outranked only by family life. Faith, for most practising Catholics, is very important.

When it comes to "means-like values" – what social psychologist Milton Rokeach years ago dubbed "instrumental" versus goal-like "terminal values"[6] – one trait stands out as valued above the rest: *honesty* (84%). People in virtually every social setting in Canada and everywhere else place high importance on honesty.

Self-reliance is valued more among Catholics (68%) than others (57%). Three other illustrative traits that we explored are seen by about 50% of Catholics as "very important": *forgiveness, concern for others* and *intellectual inquiry*. The first two are viewed as particularly important by Catholics outside Quebec – especially those who are actively involved in their parishes. (Table 4.7)

Table 4.7. Catholics and Values
% Indicating Receive "Very Important"

	ALL	CATHOLICS ROC Monthly+	ROC Less	Quebec Monthly+	Quebec Less	OTHER CANS
	(1152)	(194)	(418)	(86)	(454)	(1889)
Terminal, Goal-Like Values						
Family life	76	87	78	69	72	74
A comfortable life	51	55	61	36	43	51
Success in what you do	46	49	57	45	47	46
Spirituality	28	**60***	**21**	**43**	**17**	30
Religion	20	**64**	**9**	**39**	**7**	17
Instrumental, Means-Like Values						
Honesty	84	84	85	**74**	**86**	84
Self-reliance	68	64	68	**55**	**71**	57
Forgiveness	53	**72**	**57**	**56**	**42**	57
Concern for others	50	**66**	**54**	38	42	58
Intellectual inquiry	49	51	45	49	50	50

*** bold: difference of 10% points or more.**

Source: ARI 2015 Religion Survey.

These kinds of findings on values invariably lead to the question of the relationship between values and behaviour. Does the fact that 84% of Catholics value honesty mean that 84% of Catholics are honest? Probably not, unfortunately. Perfection is an elusive goal for any individual or group. What it does mean is that the trait has been instilled, and that seems to be a good start. After all, we can safely assume that if people are going to be honest, they need to start by valuing honesty. In philosophical terms, valuing honesty is a necessary if not sufficient condition for behaving honestly.

The same can be said for valuing a trait such as concern for others. The test obviously lies in what people actually do, not in what they say they think they should do. (Table 4.8)

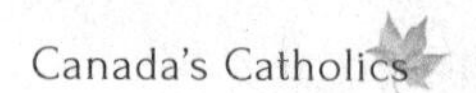

Table 4.8. Helping Behaviour

"In the last month have..."

	Donated Money to a Charity	Volunteered Time to an Organization	Helped a Stranger
ALL CATHOLICS	**50%**	**29%**	**45%**
Outside Quebec	**55**	**32**	**57**
Attend Monthly-Plus	75	54	62
Attend Less Often	45	22	54
Quebec	**44**	**26**	**33**
Attend Monthly-Plus	70	55	45
Attend Less Often	39	20	31
Other Canadians	**55**	**37**	**61**
Attend Monthly-Plus	74	59	62
Attend Less Often	50	31	61

Source: 2015 ARI Religion Survey.

Fortunately, we can do some probing, not only of values, but of behaviour as well. And we have. Our 2015 ARI Religion Survey borrowed an item from Gallup that has been administered around the world. It asks people if, in the last month, they have (1) donated money to a charity, (2) volunteered time to an organization, and (3) helped a stranger. Obviously, the measure is fairly subjective – particularly the third item. But it's a start toward tapping behaviour.

What we found is that 50% of Canada's Catholics donated money to a charity in the month before the survey was carried out. Levels were fairly similar by region and also in comparison with other Canadians.

However, active Catholics were far more likely than their inactive counterparts to have engaged in all three forms of helping behaviour. For non-Catholics, the same findings about differences by religious involvement held for donations and volunteering of time. Incidentally, Gallup has found that this pattern of the religiously involved being more likely than others to exhibit helping behaviour holds right across the planet.

Social compassion among the devout appears to be associated not only with a greater inclination to value concern for others, but also with more concerted attempts to respond to them.

All those efforts on the part of the pro-religious to encourage the faithful to "love their neighbours" appear to be having some tangible results. (Figure 4.2)

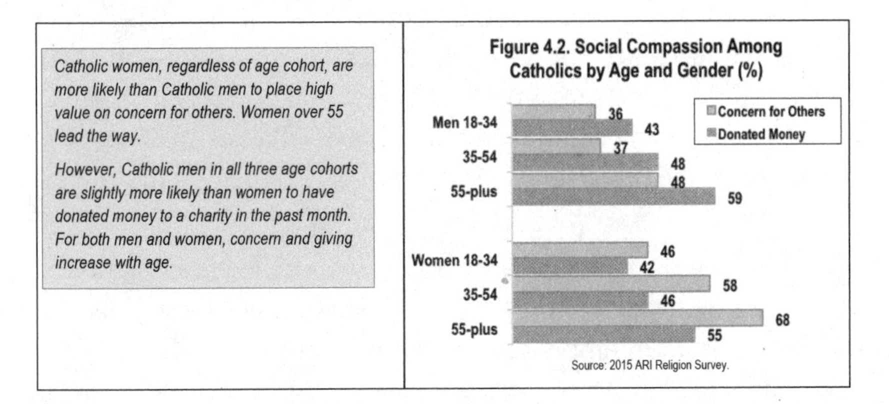

Has Social Compassion Become the Social Norm?

The 2015 ARI Religion Survey has found that 86% of Canadians agree that "people who are poor have a right to an income adequate to live on." Among Catholics and others who attend services weekly, the figure is 91%, compared to 83% for people who never attend services. That kind of finding suggests that social compassion is something that is widely valued.

However, some 71% of Canadians who attend services every week or more say that "concern for others" is very important to them, compared to 52% of people who never attend services.

Such a finding points to the fact that religious involvement contributes to the instilling of the social compassion ideal. It hardly is an exclusive source, but it is one source. The moral of the story: to the extent that Canadians are not actively involved in religious groups, some functional alternatives to religious group involvement need to be experienced if our overall societal compassion level is to be sustained.

Faith and Morality

Moral and ethical expectations are a big part of Catholicism. In sharp contrast to highly pervasive relativism, devout Catholics have guidelines that have been put in place by the Church as part of official doctrine and teachings.

Our 2015 survey explored morality with Catholics. We started by attempting to get a sense of the extent to which they believe that morality and values are linked to church involvement and God. We found that some 90% do not believe that it is necessary to go to church in order to be moral and have good values, with about 80% saying the same thing about the need to believe in God in order to be moral.

Those levels are virtually the same as those for non-Catholics. As would be expected, they are somewhat higher for non-active Catholics. What might come as a bit of a surprise is that Quebec Catholics – active or not – are less likely to agree with either statement than Catholics in the rest of Canada. That's especially true of the "not necessary to go to church" item.

Close to 75% of Catholics – led by those outside Quebec – maintain that "the Ten Commandments still apply today." Among monthly-plus attenders, the figure reaches an incredibly high 96% in "the rest of Canada" – but it also is a high 87% in Quebec.

It perhaps is very noteworthy that belief in the current applicability of the Ten Commandments among inactive Catholics remains at relatively high levels: 79% outside Quebec and 57% in Quebec. Here again we see evidence of some age-old tenets of the Christian faith being anything but abandoned by Catholics.

That's not to say inconsistencies have disappeared. Yes, some 75% of Catholics endorse the contemporary relevance of the Ten Commandments. But in the next breath, 57% agree that "what's right or wrong is a matter of personal opinion" – a level that is higher than for non-Catholics. These apparent relativists include no less than 62% of regular churchgoers in Quebec and 44% elsewhere.

On the surface, Catholics give an enthusiastic thumbs up to the Ten Commandments. Yet, having subscribed to this age-old belief in what was almost a recitation kind of style, many seem to blink and come to themselves: they endorse the prevalent idea that morality is now something that is personal and subjective, and consequently lies in the eye of the beholder. To the objective observer, more than a few Catholics seem to exhibit what might facetiously but perhaps accurately be described as "moral schizophrenia." (Table 4.9)

Table 4.9. Catholic Views on Morality (%)

	CATHOLICS					OTHER CANS
	ALL	ROC		Quebec		
		Monthly+	*Less*	*Monthly+*	*Less*	
	(1152)	(194)	(418)	(86)	(454)	(1889)
It is not necessary to "go to church" to be moral & have good values	88	79	96	69	89	89
It is not necessary to believe in God to be moral & have good values	81	71	86	66	84	82
The Ten Commandments still apply today	74	96	79	87	57	72
What's right or wrong is a matter of personal opinion	57	44	56	62	63	48

Source: ARI 2015 Religion Survey.

That ambivalence is readily apparent in the views of Catholics on specific moral questions.

- Despite the official position of the Catholic Church on sex being limited to marriage, about 1 in 3 Catholics say they approve of people having sex when they are under 18.
- Two in three Catholics approve of unmarried adults having children, even though the Church clearly specifies that children should have married parents.
- Pope Francis has called for compassion toward homosexuals, but continues to uphold the official position of the Church that homosexuality is not acceptable. Yet, close to 2 in 3 people approve both of same-sex couples marrying and their adopting children.
- And in the case of the availability of legal abortion, where the Church's position has long been opposition to any "direct attack on the fetus," no less than 85% of Catholics say that they approve of its legal possibility when a woman's health is endangered. Some 45% go much further in asserting that

a woman should be "able to obtain a legal abortion for any reason." (Table 4.10)

Table 4.10. Catholic Views on Some Specific Moral Questions
% Indicating "Approve and accept"*

	CATHOLICS					OTHER CANS
	All	ROC		Quebec		
		Monthly+	*Less*	*Monthly+*	*Less*	
	(1152)	(194)	(418)	(86)	(454)	(1889)
Unmarried people under 18 having sex	36	16	33	37	47	35
Unmarried adults having children	76	47	73	79	90	66
Same-sex couples marrying	60	38	68	62	62	66
Same-sex couples adopting children	54	39	62	56	53	63
A woman being able to obtain a legal abortion if her own health is seriously endangered by the pregnancy	85	64	88	79	93	85
A woman being able to obtain a legal abortion for any reason	45	22	51	34	52	55

*Response options: 1 Approve and accept, 2 Disapprove but accept, 3 Disapprove and do not accept.

Source: ARI 2015 Religion Survey.

Here, as with homosexuality, Pope Francis has emphasized the need for compassion. In September 2015, he extended the authority of priests worldwide to absolve women from the sin of abortion during the jubilee Year of Mercy that would begin on December 8th. "I have met so many women who bear in their heart the scar of this agonizing and painful decision," he said. "When a woman repents and seeks absolution, the forgiveness of God cannot be denied." A Vatican spokesman told reporters that the Pope's letter "highlights the wideness of God's mercy," but is "not in any way minimizing the gravity of the sin" of abortion.[7]

Catholics who are actively involved in parishes are considerably less likely than those who are inactive to approve of the availability of legal abortion, particularly those living outside Quebec. Not everyone is defying the authority of the Church.

But conformity to Catholic teachings is clearly commonly lacking, with rejection extremely rampant in Quebec.

We see here another example of the paradox that characterizes so many of Canada's Catholics. They continue to see themselves as Catholics. They are not rejecting religion. They are not about to turn elsewhere. The anomaly is not that they seem to want much, but rather that they seem to want so little. It is a difficult reality for a Church that aspires to instill commitment and participation.

The current debate on euthanasia and physician-assisted dying further illustrates the dilemma. Asked to respond to the statement "There are some circumstances in which a doctor would be justified in ending a patient's life," 79% of Catholics agree. They not only include 86% of those who attend less than monthly, but also 57% of monthly-plus attenders. Moreover, those figures are almost identical both in Quebec (87% and 59%) and in the rest of the country (85% and 56%).

These patterns are remarkably similar to what William D'Antonio and his associates have been finding in examining the beliefs, attitudes and values of American Catholics in a series of five national surveys spanning the late 1980s through now.

Such an extremely wide range of views on moral issues – even among the most devout – has led highly regarded University of Chicago historian and puzzled Protestant onlooker Martin Marty to see the diverse takes as evidence of "contemporary bi-polar Catholicism."[8] Trust us: he means that respectfully.

In addition, in all of their surveys, they have found that *three variables* have stood out as being associated with embracing or not embracing church teachings: *generation* (older versus younger), *gender* (women versus men) and *commitment to the Church.*[9] We will continue to keep an eye on such variations as we look at our findings for Canada.

Canadian Catholic Survey Bytes

% Indicating "Approve and Accept"

	Premarital Sex Under 18	Same-sex Marriage	Legal Abortion for Any Reason
ALL	**36%**	**60%**	**45%**
18–34	55	76	54
35–54	39	61	38
55+	21	49	36
Women	32	71	49
Men	40	48	41

American Catholics: A Mirror on the Wall?

Catholics strongly subscribe to the principles of religious freedom and conscience and have long made up their own minds about where they stand regarding the morality of contraception, abortion, same-sex and nonmarital sexual morality, and issues of marriage and divorce.

Catholics are open to taking account of church teachings, but the majority reserve for themselves the responsibility to be the final moral arbiter of right and wrong. Although the Vatican and the bishops continue to insist on their singular teaching authority, derived from Jesus through Peter and his successors, many lay Catholics value personal autonomy and conscience as highly or higher on some teachings.

At the same time, they also indicate that Catholicism and the Church are integral to their identity. Eighty-eight percent said that it is unlikely that they would ever leave the Catholic Church.

William D'Antonio, Michele Dillon, and Mary L. Gautier, *American Catholics in Transition*, 2013. K1490, 1491, 1501, 936.
Summary of findings for a series of national surveys of U.S. Catholics carried out in 1987, 1993, 1999, 2005, 2011.

Part of the positive response to Pope Francis that we saw earlier seems to be tied to the fact that he has been seen by many Catholics as the kind of Pope they had hoped for. In early 2013, about 10 days before his election, Angus Reid Public Opinion surveyed some 1,200 Canadian and 1,200 American Catholics. The two samples were evenly divided between those who attended services at least once a week and those who attended less often.[10] They were asked about the kind of pontiff they would like to see chosen. (Table 4.11)

Table 4.11. Views Concerning Pope Benedict's Successor: Canadian and American Catholics by Attendance (%)

	CANADA		UNITED STATES	
	Weekly Plus (602)	Less Often (605)	Weekly Plus (604)	Less Often (608)
He should be a pontiff who is...				
very liberal/has liberal leanings	60	69	47	51
centrist	13	12	21	18
very conservative/has conservative leanings	20	11	20	14
not sure	7	9	12	16
He should be a pontiff who takes a more liberal approach to...				
contraception/birth control	57	77	43	59
divorce	43	59	35	47
same-sex relations	34	56	24	40
euthanasia/doctor-assisted suicide	18	48	17	29
He "definitely" or "probably should"...				
allow women to be ordained	62	81 52	71	
allow priests to get married	71	82 55	68	

Source: Angus Reid Public Opinion Release, March 11, 2013.

The participants also were asked whether the new Pope should take "a more liberal approach, a more conservative approach, or leave things as they are" with respect to contraception, divorce, same-sex relations and euthanasia. In addition, they were asked if "the next pontiff should implement" policies that would "allow women to become ordained" and "allow priests to get married."

Clearly most Catholics – active and otherwise – hoped that the next Pope would have liberal leanings, with large numbers – led by the less active – wanting him to take a more liberal approach on contraception and permitting women to be ordained and priests to marry. Catholics in both countries were highly divided, however, on divorce and same-sex relations, and not very inclined to want the next pontiff to support euthanasia. Overall, Canadian Catholics – active or not – were much more likely than their American counterparts to want a liberally minded Pope. In Francis, many got their wish.

Faith and Social Relations

The complexity and diversity of Catholic identification is found in the responses of people to twin statements:

I feel a bit uncomfortable around people who are religiously devout.

I feel a bit uncomfortable around people who have no use for religion.

About 1 in 3 Catholics agree that they are somewhat uncomfortable around the devout. At the same time, 1 in 4 say they are somewhat uncomfortable around people with no use for religion.

If Catholics were simply *pro-religious* or *not religious* based on an indicator like attendance, we could expect that the comfort levels would be fairly predictable. What makes things a bit confusing is that a lot of Catholics who seem to not care much about faith actually do. Consequently, there are an array of sentiments that Catholics as a whole have toward people they encounter who are variously devout and overtly non-devout. Just ask yourself how many a "latent Catholic" would respond if some loudmouth started bad-mouthing the Pope....

One window for viewing that complexity is to look at the attitudes Catholics have toward people who are variously devout and non-devout by their inclination to embrace religion (35%), reject it (15%) or be ambivalent (50%). (Table 4.12)

Table 4.12. Catholics and Comfort Around the Devout and Non-Devout

% Agreeing

	ALL (1152)	Embrace (402)	Ambivalent (583)	Reject (167)
I feel a bit uncomfortable around people who are religiously devout	34	22	37	53
I feel a bit uncomfortable around people who have no use for religion	23	38	17	8

Source: ARI 2015 Religion Survey.

What we find is that some Catholics who embrace faith or are ambivalent toward it are among those who feel comfortable around people who *are* devout. Similarly, some who are ambivalent about their own faith are uncomfortable around people who have no use for religion, as are even about 1 in 10 Catholics who are inclined to *reject religion*. Folks who are Catholic are not exactly a monolithic bunch.

In examining attitudes toward religious groups, we provided our survey participants with a fairly thorough (if hardly exhaustive) list of 10 fairly prominent Canadian groups, including Atheists. We asked them to indicate "how positive, neutral, or negative" they feel toward each.

What we found is that, for all our celebrations about our diversity and inclusiveness, we still have a good distance to go before we can claim we have reached a pluralistic utopia when it comes to our diverse religious – and non-religious – groups.

On the contrary, forgetting about Catholics for the moment, Canadians who are not Catholic exhibit negative feelings toward religious groups that range from a low of 9% for Protestants to a high of 41% for Muslims. Some 19% acknowledge that they have negative feelings toward Canada's Catholics.

And let no one be so naïve as to assume that people who have no religion are particularly neutral toward specific religious groups. Some 24% admit they have negative feelings about Catholics, 38% feel negative about Muslims, and close to half (44%) admit they feel negative about evangelical Christians. (Table 4.13)

Table 4.13. Catholics and Feelings Toward Other Groups
"How positive, neutral, or negative do you feel toward the following groups?"
% Indicating Negative

	ALL	CATHOLICS ROC Monthly+		QUEBEC Monthly+		OTHER CANS	NO RELIG
		Monthly+	Less	Monthly+	Less		
	(1152)	(194)	(418)	(86)	(454)	(1889)	(510)
Roman Catholics	4	3	4	8	3	19	24
Protestants	7	4	6	7	9	9	14
Buddhists	8	9	6	14	9	10	7
Hindus	12	7	13	19	13	18	15
Jews	13	6	8	14	20	11	15
Evangelical Christians	18	19	20	16	15	32	44
Atheists	22	39	20	28	15	22	6
Sikhs	27	17	23	41	33	26	24
Mormons	30	17	28	40	36	38	42
Muslims	49	29	42	55	63	41	38
Average Score	***19***	***15***	***17***	***24***	***22***	***23***	***23***

Source: ARI 2015 Religion Survey.

Getting back to Catholics, it's interesting to see that few – inactive or active – are explicitly negative about Catholics.

- Protestants, Buddhists, Hindus and Jews are all "favoured groups" – although Catholics in Quebec exhibit some negativism toward Jews.
- Negative views of groups increase to 18% for Evangelical Christians and to 22% for atheists. In both cases, such sentiments are slightly higher outside Quebec. Some 30% of Catholics, led by those in Quebec, express negative feelings toward Mormons.

Principles for Interfaith Dialogue and Interfaith Attitudes

We live inside a world and inside religions that are too given to disrespect and violence. Virtually every newscast today documents the prevalence of disrespect and violence done in the name of religion. And, if history is to be believed, it has always been so. No religion, Christianity no less than any other, has been innocent.

So this begs the question: What are some fundamental principles we are asked to live out apposite our relationship to other faiths, irrespective our particular faith? Perhaps the issue of religious diversity might be described in this way:

Different peoples, one earth. Different beliefs, one God. Different languages, one heart. Different failings, one law of gravity.

Different energies, one Spirit. Different scriptures, one Word. Different forms of worship, one desire. Different histories, one destiny. Different disciplines, one aim. Different approaches, one road.

Different faiths – one Mother, one Father, one earth, one sky, one beginning, one end.

Ron Rolheiser, OMI, column of April 13, 2015.

- But the highest level of negativism is directed towards Muslims, with those sentiments much higher in Quebec than in the rest of the country – where they nonetheless are also relatively high. They seem clearly tied to concerns about violence.

Negative views of groups are typically more prevalent among inactive than active Catholics. But that pattern is not consistent in Quebec.

One can rightfully point out that it is also clear from these findings that negative feelings are not just "one way" – that religious polarization is also seeing a fair amount of hostility toward the devout on the part of people who are rejecting religion. But that doesn't provide those who value faith with an exemption. Gregory Baum has reminded us that Catholic theology calls for "the honouring of different faiths and the rejoicing in religious pluralism." But he also points out that the sacred "can be used to promote good and evil, peace and war," adding, "Religion is truly a mixed bag."[11]

These findings show that there is still much work to do in cultivating "joy in diversity." In keeping with the poignant advice of Pope Francis during his Cuban visit, more than a few of us who are different from each other "need to talk."[12] (Figure 4.3)

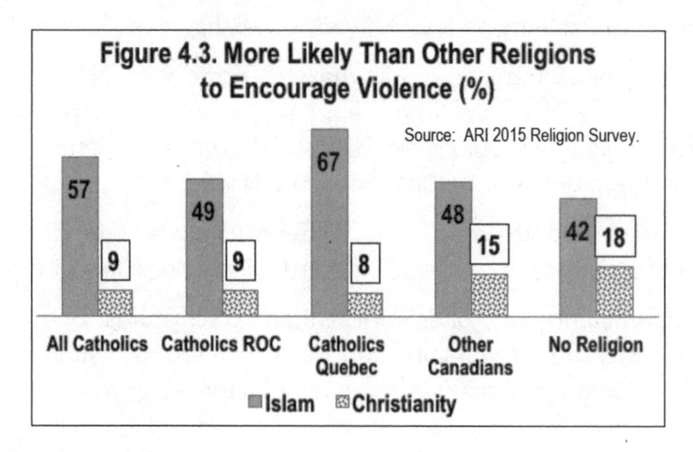

Faith and Politics

Dating back to at least the 1960s, political scientists have found that Canadian Catholics – particularly those in Quebec – have tended to favour the Liberal party.[13] The dominant explanation is that Catholics, often having experienced conditions of disadvantage, particularly in Quebec, have seen their best chances for enhanced living with less status quo–oriented parties than the Conservatives.[14] (Table 4.14)

Table 4.14. Political Party Preference of Canadian Catholics

	1975			1995			2015		
	ALL	ROC	QC	ALL	ROC	QC	ALL	ROC	QC
Liberal	59%	58%	60%	52%	63%	41%	21%	26%	16%
Conservative	12	23	3	11	16	7	35	49	19
NDP	17	16	17	5	9	2	25	18	33
Bloc Québécois *est 1991*	---	---	---	25	1	47	12	<1	25
Other	12	3	20	7	11	3	7	6	7
Total	100	100	100	100	100	100	100	100	100

*1975 and 1995: party preference; 2015 party voted for in last federal election.

Sources: Reginald W. Bibby, 1975 and 1995 Project Canada national surveys, and ARI 2015 Religion Survey.

In parallel fashion, researchers in the U.S. have found that Catholics have historically favoured the "average person" Democratic party over the establishment-leaning Republicans.[15] Elsewhere, the pattern is similar: in countries where Catholics have been disadvantaged – Great Britain, Australia and New Zealand – they have tended to identify with liberal parties. In countries where Catholics are not disadvantaged, they have leaned toward conservative parties.[16]

Those patterns are fairly readily evident in Canada from an examination of party preferences in 1975 and 1995, along with federal party voting in 2015. With social parity, such differences in political party preferences would be expected to diminish – and have done so significantly, especially outside Quebec. But the ongoing presence of large numbers of immigrants may mean that many of Canada's Catholics will continue to gravitate toward parties other than the Conservatives for some time to come.

And When All's Said and Done…

Asked what they see as the key determinants of what takes place in their lives, some 8 in 10 Catholics and other Canadians emphasize two factors: their own efforts and their health.

But as we look more closely at Catholics who are involved in their parishes, we find that in both "the rest of Canada" and Quebec, God is included along with those two primary factors. God is also cited as a key determinant of life by some 3 in 10 people who are not religiously active.

We all know that another important source of what happens in our lives is other people. Life isn't lived in a social vacuum. About 1 in 2 Catholics and others acknowledge the importance of "the human factor."

Beyond these sources, some 4 in 10 Catholics and others maintain that two additional key determinants of what takes place are chance and luck. Many people concede that the things that unfold in life are not necessarily always predictable or rational. As we all know, outcomes sometimes do not have clear-cut cause and effect sequences. They just happen – reflecting chance and luck, or the lack of it.[17]

In short, for practising Catholics – regardless of where they are located – God is a factor that they see as being as important as their own efforts and health in determining life. This blunt and succinct admission is key to understanding the role of faith in the lives of Canada's Catholics. In Thomas Groome's words, "at its best, Catholic Christianity is a tremendous way to live humanly, religiously, and Christianly. It's a rich resource for growing into fullness of life as a person of God after the way of Jesus – and a lot of fun besides."[18] (Table 4.15)

Table 4.15. Catholics and Key Life Determinants

"To what extent do you see your life as determined by..."

% Indicating "A Great Deal" or "Quite a Bit"

	CATHOLICS					OTHER CANS
	ALL	ROC		Quebec		
		Monthly+	*Less*	*Monthly+*	*Less*	
	(1152)	(194)	(418)	(86)	(454)	(1889)
Your own efforts	92	83	91	77	83	88
Your health	88	77	83	85	90	81
Other people	48	47	41	57	50	43
God	44	82	26	78	29	36
Chance	44	27	40	48	49	37
Luck	37	20	32	46	43	30

Source: ARI 2015 Religion Survey.

So there we have it… a Church that numerically is mighty, that predates the founding of the country and will be there as far into the future as we can see, because its large Canadian nucleus will continued to be filled out by people from around the world.

With its present and future ensured, it now needs to turn its sights on where more precisely things are headed, and what kind of Church it wants – and needs – to be.

We'll turn to those important questions now.

5

Where Things Are Headed

The Bright Future for Catholicism in Canada

Don't fear for the future of the Catholic faith in Canada.

Many key features should be readily apparent by now. Catholics are easily the largest religious group in every region of the country. The vast majority of Catholics remain Catholic intergenerationally. And what's more, because of the prominence of the Catholic Church worldwide, the immigration pipeline has brought, is bringing and will continue to bring large numbers of new Catholics to Canada from all around the globe into the foreseeable future. (Table 5.1)

Table 5.1. Religious Groups: 2011
In 1000s

Roman Catholic	12,811	39%
Everyone else	12,190	37
No Religion	7,851	24

Source: 2011 National Household Survey.

All in all, a pretty enviable organizational situation.

Current Parish Patterns

Observers are constantly talking about the decline in congregations of all kinds, including Catholic parishes. We asked Catholics and other Canadians who are involved in congregations about the actual numerical patterns they are experiencing, using this straightforward question: "*In recent years, has your religious group or congregation been growing, declining, or staying about the same?*"

There is considerable parish vitality outside Quebec. Three in 10 Catholics say their congregations have been growing, and 5 in 10 say that they have been staying about the same; just 2 in 10 say they have been declining. In Quebec, it's a somewhat different story – but perhaps not as different as some pessimists think. Just 1 in 10 people say their churches have been growing and more than 3 in 10 say they have been declining. Still, close to 7 in 10 maintain that they have been staying about the same

In short, these self-reports point to considerable life across the country. It's far from a perfect growth story, but neither is it a progress report that warrants excessive gloom and doom.

For the record, Canadians who are not Catholic are even more buoyant about what has been happening in their congregations in recent years. Some 4 in 10 say they have been growing, and almost another 4 in 10 that they have remained about the same. Just 2 in 10 report that their groups have been declining. (Table 5.2)

Table 5.2. Numerical Patterns in Catholic Parishes

"In recent years, has your religious group or congregation been growing, declining, or staying about the same?"

Views Offered by Monthly-Plus Attenders (%)

	CATHOLICS			OTHER
	ALL (280)	ROC (193)	Quebec (86)	CANS (407)
Growing	25	30	10	42
Declining	25	21	34	22
Staying about the same	50	49	56	36
TOTALS	100	100	100	100

Source: 2015 ARI Religion Survey.

All in all, not exactly a national picture of congregations in demise.

Size-wise, the number of people involved in Catholic parishes typically is much higher than those who are associated with non-Catholic congregations.

- Just 3 in 10 Catholics are in parishes with less than 150 active members, compared to some 5 in 10 people who are not Catholic.
- At the other end of the size spectrum, 3 in 10 Catholics are part of parishes with more than 750 active members, compared to just 1 in 10 non-Catholics.

The size situation signals both opportunity and challenge: large parishes point to lots of Catholics. But it also means significant human and financial resources are needed to adequately respond to them. (Table 5.3)

Table 5.3. Numbers in Catholic Parishes

"Approximately how many people are actively involved in your religious group or congregation?"

Estimates Provided by Monthly-Plus Attenders*

	CATHOLICS (279)	OTHER CANS (360)
Under 50 people	11%	16%
51–150	20	32
151–350	18	24
351–500	9	13
501–750	11	5
751–1000	9	4
1001–2000	9	2
Over 2000 people	13	4

*Additional unsure: Catholics 77; Other Canadians 48.

Source: 2015 ARI Religion Survey.

Geographical Variations in Involvement

We saw in chapter 3 that the largest number of Canada's 13 million Catholics live in two provinces – Quebec (5.8 million) and Ontario (4 million). That works out to about 75% of all Catholics. They also have a noteworthy numerical presence in the other provinces and territories, despite the fact that their individual numerical shares in the Church range from only about 7% to less than 1%.

With respect to parish involvement, Statistics Canada data provided by the annual General Social Survey (GSS) – a mammoth initiative that typically includes samples of 20,000 Canadians or more – provides us with a reliable snapshot of Catholic attendance across the country.

- The most recent GSS (2012) shows that, nationally, weekly-plus Catholic attendance is just under 20%, with monthly-plus attendance about 30%.
- Weekly attendance is highest for Catholics in British Columbia (around 30%), slightly lower for people on the Prairies and in the Atlantic area (some 25%; a bit lower in New Brunswick) and lowest in Quebec (about 10%).
- Monthly-plus attendance levels are fairly similar from Ontario to B.C. (some 40%), somewhat lower in the Atlantic region, with the exception of PEI, and lowest in Quebec (around 15%). (Figure 5.1)

Figure 5.1. Attend Weekly or More and Monthly or More (%)

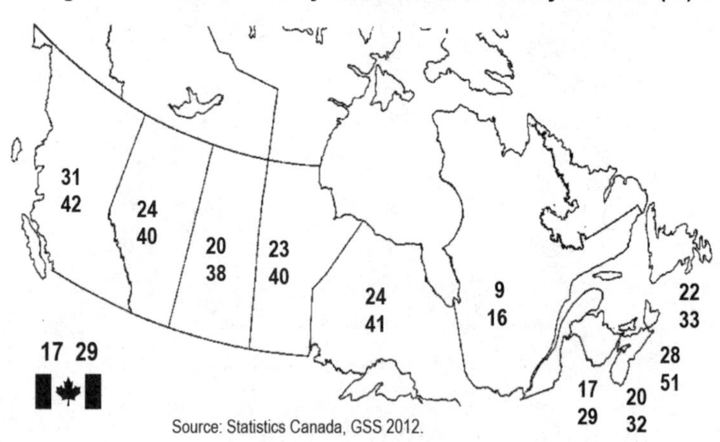

Social Variations in Involvement

In keeping with widespread perception, people present for mass can be expected to be somewhat older: the 2012 GSS tells us that close to 40% of Catholics 55 and older say they attend mass at least once a month. But that age cohort hardly worships alone: 25% of Catholics who are 35 to 54 also claim they attend services once a month or more, as do about 20% of adults under 35. Weekly figures are obviously lower, but follow similar age patterns.

Catholic *women* are slightly more inclined than Catholic *men* to attend services at least once a month. The differences, however, are fairly small. Nationally, worshippers should find that, in most parish settings, the people present at a typical mass are just about as likely to be male as female.

Canadian Catholic Survey Bytes

Monthly-Plus Attendance by Age, Education, Gender, and Birthplace

18–34	21%	**Degree-plus**	28%
35–54	25	**Some post-secondary**	23
55+	38	**High school or less**	23
Women	32	**Born in Canada**	24
Men	26	**Born outside Canada**	55

Source: Statistics Canada, GSS 2012.

Catholic attendance differs very little by education.

And what about the *immigration* factor? As we saw earlier, Catholics who have come from other countries are considerably more likely than those born in Canada to be attending services (55% versus 24%). Allowing for the fact that more than 80% of Catholics were born in Canada, the quick math tells us that, nationally, on a given weekend, the pews in Catholic parishes are being occupied by 2 in 3 people from Canada, and 1 in 3 from other countries. In Ontario cities, says StatsCan, that ratio is almost exactly 50:50. This is increasingly a global Church.

To be more precise, the pews where immigrants are sitting are not always in the existing churches of other Canadians – although frequently groups like Filipinos, in particular, who feel a high level of cultural affinity with North Americans, can be seen in parish gatherings where Caucasians are in the majority.

In many cases, immigrants are part of parishes where they constitute the numerical majorities. Across the country, a sizable number of such parishes – particularly some that are Asian – have been growing fairly dramatically, becoming what Protestants in particular often dub as "megachurches," with more than 1,000 people attending services on a given weekend.[1]

Some Specific Variations in Immigration Additions

An Illustrative View of Asian Catholic Parishes across the Country

CHINESE	
• St. Francis Xavier, Vancouver	founded 1933, new facilities 2008, 2,000 members, 600 families, 20 ministries
• Canadian Martyrs, Richmond, BC	founded 1995, new facility 2003, 1,200 registered families
• Our Lady of Perpetual Help, Calgary	founded 1981, 4,000 members
• Our Lady of Mount Carmel, Toronto	structure founded 1861, home of Chinese Catholics 1970
• Chinese Martyrs, Markham	founded 1988, new facility 1994, 1,000 at typical mass
FILIPINO	
• St. Patrick's, Vancouver	75% of its 3,000 families are Filipino
• St. Paul's, Richmond, BC	multicultural parish, 8,000 members, a large percentage are Filipino
• St. Peter's, Winnipeg	85% of congregation is Filipino
• Blessed John XXIII, Toronto	50% of its 3,000 parishioners are Filipino
• Filipino Catholic Mission of Montreal	founded 1989, moved to refurbished Catholic church in 2006,1,500 parishioners
KOREAN	
• St. Andrew Kim, Surrey	established 2001, community of 6,500
• St. Anne's, Calgary	founded 1982, community of 2,500
• St. Andrew Kim, Toronto	founded 1981, 7,000 members
VIETNAMESE	
• St. Joseph, Vancouver	6,100 members
• St. Joseph, Port Moody, BC	2,700 parishioners
• Queen of Martyrs, Edmonton	founded 1994, 750 members
• Vietnamese Martyrs, Toronto	established 1986, 5,300 members
• Vietnamese Martyrs, Montreal	founded 1979, 700 members

Sources: Terence J. Fay, *New Faces of Canadian Catholics*, 2009; parish and other relevant websites.

We have been emphasizing the importance that immigration has played and will continue to play in Catholic growth. But the impact of people arriving from elsewhere is far from uniform.

- Some 56% of foreign-born Catholics are living in Ontario, including some 50% of younger immigrants under the age of 35.
- Quebec and the four western provinces – led by British Columbia and Alberta – are well behind Ontario, but still numerically important destinations of immigrants.
- Well behind is the Atlantic region.

These are the parts of Canada that, in the immediate future, are going to be affected the most by the influx of people from around the world. (Figure 5.2; Table 5.4)

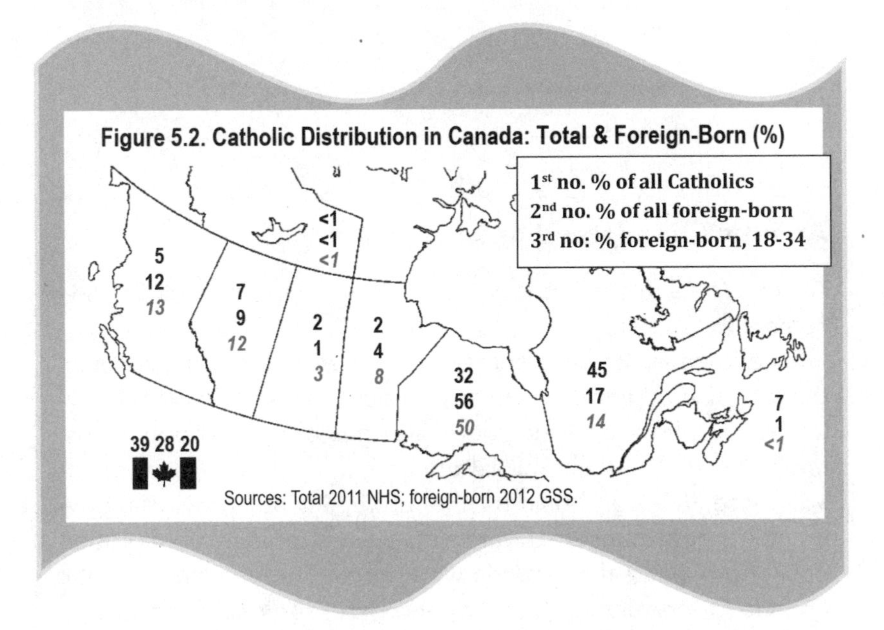

Figure 5.2. Catholic Distribution in Canada: Total & Foreign-Born (%)

Table 5.4. Destinations of Immigrants: Observed and Projected

Annual Number In 1000s

	2008–2009	2035–2036
NATIONALLY	**245**	**334**
Ontario	107	166
British Columbia	42	61
Quebec	46	53
Alberta	24	30
Manitoba	13	13
Saskatchewan	6	4
Nova Scotia	2	3
New Brunswick	2	2
Prince Edward Island	2	1
Newfoundland-Labrador	<1	<1
Yukon	<1	<1
Northwest Territories	<1	<1
Nunavut	<1	<1

Source: Derived from Statistics Canada Demography Division, 2012: Cat. No. 91-520-X. Table 1.4, Medium Assumption.

Atlantic Canada and newcomers

Atlantic Canada traditionally has not seen large influxes of newcomers to Canada.

Recent initiatives have somewhat altered this trend. However, the rate of immigration is not high enough to satisfy regional governments, who are facing the challenges of aging populations, low birth rates, and chronic labour shortages. To effectively manage these issues and plan for the future, Atlantic provincial governments have banded together to build a regional immigration policy to expand the Atlantic work force. Through [the Atlantic Canada Opportunities Agency], and other regional initiatives to promote Atlantic Canada as an immigration destination, Atlantic cities have seen significant increases in the number of newcomers. Immigrant communities are reaching critical masses in many of Atlantic Canada's cities.

Source: CanadaVisa.com

The demographic staff at Statistics Canada tell us that, by around 2035, we can expect that the areas of Canada that will be receiving the largest number of immigrants – including Catholics – will be essentially the same areas as now: Ontario, followed by B.C. and Alberta, along with Manitoba and Saskatchewan.

Keep in mind that immigrants are typically younger than the host population, meaning that they also are more inclined to be either single or married with young families. They will be breathing new life into Catholic parishes, and will require ministries that are in touch with their demographical makeup. That in turn will require noteworthy increases in facilities and personnel.

It will be no mean feat to stay ahead of the surge in the Catholic population. And to think that the social science prophets of a century ago saw so little of this coming!

The Canadian Religious Market in 2050

The religious situation in Canada by the middle part of this century will be anything but what many people were forecasting in the last part of the 20th century.

As we have been emphasizing, the majority of academics, religious leaders, folks in the media and others were telling everyone that religion was on its last legs. In 1975, renowned CBC journalist Barbara Frum applied the sentiment of the day as she began an interview with one of us on our research findings: "Organized religion in Canada is on the skids."[2] For many who valued faith and the Church, it was neither a pretty nor an uplifting picture.

It turns out that those who kept their cameras running have found that the religion game was only halfway through the first period. Now, in what may only be the second period, it is clear that religion is thriving worldwide, was never dying in Canada, and continues to know considerable vitality. A handful of previously stellar players have been relegated to the bench. But the game goes on.

An extremely important, well-researched document on religious group size projections for countries around the world was released by the highly reputable Pew Research Center in the United States in April of 2015. Canada, of course, was included.[3]

Pew maintains that Canadians identifying themselves as Christians – now some 70% – will slip to about 60% by 2050. The decline will not be because increasingly large numbers are opting for "No Religion," but rather because of the growth of other major world faiths. Christians will still be the choice of a large majority of Canadians by mid-century.

So much for the talk about the demise of religion in general, and Christianity and Catholicism in particular. Religion's future in Canada is not in question. By 2050, some 6 in 10 people will identify with the Christian faith. That represents a huge religious market. The primary question is not "Will there be a religious market?" but rather "What groups will step up and service that market?" (Table 5.5)

Table 5.5. Current and Projected Sizes of Major Religious Groups in Canada: 2010 to 2050

	2010	2030	2050
1. Christians	69%	64%	60%
2. No Religion	24	25	26
3. Muslims	2	4	6
4. Hindus	1	2	3
5. Buddhists	1	1	2
6. Jews	1	1	1
7. Other	2	3	2

Source: Pew Research Center, 2015. *The Future of World Religions: Population Growth Projections, 2010–2050.*

The majority of that 60% will see themselves as Catholic. Guess who needs to step up?

What an opportunity! What a responsibility!

You know what is needed next.

6

What's Needed by Way of a Response

Catholics in the twenty-first century won't just need hustle, but above all they will need imagination. They'll need the capacity to reconsider how they think about the Church, and what they do with their faith, because otherwise Catholicism won't rise to the occasion of these new challenges – it'll be steamrolled by them.

—John L. Allen Jr., 2009

We are hardly so audacious as to think we have all the answers with respect to what comes next.

But we do have some informed reflections, thanks primarily to a lot of conversations with Catholics. Over the years, we have spoken with many church leaders and active laity. Our surveys have also allowed us to have conversations with a large number of average Catholics across the country, from the highly involved to those who are no longer involved, including a good number whose Catholic tie is only a precarious thread that goes back to their mothers and fathers. We also have had many opportunities to exchange ideas with Catholics face to face in the course of presenting our findings across the country.

On a personal note, Angus is a Catholic who has been highly involved in Catholic life, particularly over the past few decades. Reg's wife and young daughter are Catholic, and Sahara – now 13 – has been in the Catholic school system all of her life.

In addition, we are not lost for ideas of our own as to where things might go from here. We hope that what follows will stimulate thought but will also do much more, namely, contribute to concrete efforts to enhance ministry and thereby enhance the lives of Catholics and others.

Our data tell us a great deal about where Canada's Catholics are. A major initial question that church leaders need to address is where they want to go from here: what do they want to accomplish?

If a Major Goal is Greater Involvement...

We assume that, for many readers, a major goal is increased involvement and in turn a greater level of commitment on the part of Catholics. To the extent that this is the case, a good starting point is to get a sense of how open people are to such a possibility.

In our 2015 survey, we put the question to Catholics and others. We asked them to respond to the statement "*I'd be open to more involvement with religious groups if I found it worthwhile.*"

Nationally, almost 4 in 10 Catholics agreed. They are led by people who are already attending services monthly or more. Yet, in addition, more than 3 in 10 individuals who attend only yearly, and 2 in 10 who acknowledge they never attend services, indicate that they too are receptive to being more involved. (Table 6.1)

Table 6.1. Receptivity to Greater Involvement

"I'd be open to more involvement with religious groups if I found it worthwhile."

% Agreeing

	Totals	Weekly	Monthly	Yearly	Never
ALL CATHOLICS	37	54	58	34	21
Outside Quebec	50	54	63	51	35
Quebec	21	52	50	18	8

Source: 2015 ARI Religion Survey.

Regionally, Catholics outside Quebec (50%) are far more likely than those in Quebec (21%) to say they are open to greater participation. In Quebec, signs of receptivity are predictably low among those who seldom (18%) or never (8%) attend.

Age variations are not as great as many might think. In fact, somewhat surprisingly, the findings point to considerable openness to greater involvement on the part of younger Catholics.

- Outside Quebec, some 60% of people 18 to 34 indicated receptivity – led by a slightly higher proportion of males than females. That level compares to 50% for Catholics who are 35 to 54 years old, and about 20% of those who are over 55. The message: older Catholics have tended to "settle in" when it comes to participation; younger Catholics, led by males, have not.
- In Quebec, receptivity levels for people in all three age cohorts are considerable lower and vary little by age. That said, there is a measure of openness among younger adults, especially young women.

Table 6.2. Catholic Receptivity by Age, Gender and Region

"I'd be open to more involvement with religious groups if I found it worthwhile."

% Agreeing

	ALL	ROC	QUEBEC
ALL	**37**	**50**	**21**
18–34	46	62	25
35–54	35	50	18
55+	32	42	22
Men	**40**	**57**	**22**
18–34	43	63	17
35–54	38	56	21
55+	40	54	27
Women	**33**	**44**	**20**
18–34	49	61	34
35–54	31	45	15
55+	26	33	18

Source: 2015 ARI Religion Survey.

The good news here for those who want to see greater levels of involvement of Catholics is that the market for greater participation is extensive. Outside Quebec, the possibility is there in the case of as many as 5 in 10 people. But even in Quebec, at least 2 in 10 Catholics also are receptive to being more actively involved – including some 1 in 3 women and 1 in 5 men under the age of 35.

What Will It Take?

This general finding that Catholics and other people across the country have not shut the door on greater involvement is something we have been seeing in our surveys now for a number of years.

For example, in his Project Canada national surveys in 1995, 2000 and 2005, Bibby asked Canadians, "*Would you consider the possibility of being more involved in a religious group if you found it to be worthwhile for yourself or your family?*" He found that some 50% to 60% of Catholics who were attending services less than once a month responded either "Yes" or "Perhaps."[1] The fact that the initial figure in 1995 was so high came as a surprise – leading him to wish he had followed up the item by asking the obvious question: what would people would see as "worthwhile"?

The 2000 and 2005 surveys, asked the additional question "*What kinds of things would make it worthwhile?*" Responses were open-ended.

The results were consistent and, we believe, are still pertinent. Respondents emphasized the need for relevant ministry that elevates their lives and the lives of their families; for caring and trustworthy churches and parishes that value diversity and inclusion. Many also acknowledged that their lack of involvement sometimes does not reflect dissatisfaction with groups but rather is associated with personal factors such as scheduling, aging and lack of relational support.

These findings suggest that many Catholics and other Canadians are open to the possibility of greater involvement. But they have to find that their participation is worthwhile – adding something to their lives and to the lives of the people they care most about. To the extent they fail to find such significance, Catholics – like everyone else – can be expected to take a pass on religious involvement. (Table 6.3)

Table 6.3. What Would Make Greater Involvement Worthwhile

Key Factors Cited by Catholics Attending <Monthly Who Are Receptive (N=121)

Ministry Factors	**41%**
Specific ministries	17
Personal interests & needs	13
Society-oriented	6
God and spirituality	5
Organizational Factors	**23**
Changes in style and outlook	19
Better leadership	4
Ministry Qualities	**18**
Relevant, realistic	6
Integrity, genuine, authentic	5
Interesting, stimulating, lively	2
Caring, helpful	5
Respondent Factors	**18**
Schedule changes	10
Involvement of family & friends	4
Getting older, children, health, etc.	3
Other	1
Total	**100**

Source: Bibby, Project Canada 2005 National Survey.

Do you recall the finding that we discussed briefly in chapter 3 about the expectations of Canada's Catholics, where 66% said that their parents felt that they were "supposed to go to church," whereas 72% maintain that people today "should not go because they feel they have to but because they find it to be worthwhile"?

For better or for worse, that's the mindset of a majority of Catholics these days. Most are not looking for churches; they are looking for good ministry. The proverbial bottom line? "Don't tell people they need to go to church." Increasingly, the response will be, "Why?"

Pragmatism and practicality rule today. That's not to say people aren't willing to give of themselves. But they have to believe that their lives and the people they care most about are better for the expenditure of time and money. They have to find that involvement is worthwhile.

In cold marketing language, the future of religious participation in Canada will depend largely on the ability of "religious companies" to provide what people believe they need. Such success on the "supply side" obviously is not a sufficient cause that guarantees organizational success. Nonetheless, the contribution of the supply side is a necessary cause. Everyone will not respond; but without the supply, why would anyone bother with organized religion?[2]

The good news for Catholicism in Canada is that significant numbers of people continue to indicate that they are open to some of the life-enhancing things that the Church can bring.

And then there is the anomaly of Quebec.

The Quebec Enigma

Dictionaries variously define "enigma" as "puzzling," "inexplicable," "perplexing," and so on. You get the fuzzy picture – and here we are not talking about "warm and fuzzy...."

The Marginals: What People Say Would Make Greater Involvement Worthwhile

Ministry Factors

...It would have to add value to my life...more family things... spiritual guidance related to everyday living and practices...get to know the people in my community better...for my family's well-being...if it was uplifting and added to life...emphasis on the love of God, caring about others, etc. rather than the pomp, ceremony and ritual...programs for children...sermons given by a good speaker that are upbeat.... →

Organizational Factors
...Get away from the boring traditional ways and change with the times...a non-judgmental environment that emphasizes spiritual development rather than rules...accept things that are different, such as gay marriage and choice decisions, and offer women a greater role...if the sermons were more relevant to today...a priest that you can understand...no talk of heaven or hell....

Ministry Qualities
...A community of faith that is genuine and caring...more up-to-date and relevant sermons, good music, and more local involvement...honesty, a group that really did practise what they preached...more age-appropriate things for teenagers and young adult groups...services that I am able to get something from...dealing with the real-life issues of today...some vitality and positive energy....

Personal Factors
...I see myself attending my church again on a regular basis, but right now my life is congested and I have little time for anything else...if I had children and my partner wanted to expose them to religion, it would make my in-laws happy...if my spouse wanted to go...if someone in the family got something out of it...make it Sunday afternoon, not morning...if it could have a positive influence on my partner and our children...I need more time....

Source: Drawn from Bibby, *Canadian Review of Sociology,* 2012.

We already have provided the data and made the point that the difficulty the Catholic Church has in Quebec is not one of too few Catholics. For all the talk about defection, identification with the Catholic Church in the province remains highly pervasive. What's more, the intergenerational data point to a remarkably high level of retention. Catholics continue to beget Catholics.

Those people who identify with the faith to varying degrees believe and practise and experience religion à la carte, Catholic-style, including wanting rites of passage and valuing occasional, seasonal attendance. They are not about to turn anywhere else for their religion.

But most do not want a lot from the faith, nor – it seems – are they prepared to give a lot. Detractors may variously refer to the majority of Quebec Catholics as "inactive," "indifferent," "freeloaders," in need of "the new evangelism" or, in the case of Protestant evangelicals, in need of "the old evangelism." Regardless, they remain Catholic – faithful to the tradition if not to the faith. The title of Konrad Yakabuski's overview article in *The Globe and Mail* in August 2009 sums up the situation well: "Neither practising nor believing, but Catholic even so."[3]

Thomas Groome's reflections on many American Catholics seem highly applicable to a good number of Canada's Catholics in Quebec and elsewhere. Leaving a local church, he says, "is easy compared to erasing the traces of Catholic socialization." It has shaped them in many ways: "their values, virtues, and vices, their hopes and fears, even their sense of humor." In his poetic language, they commonly cherish their "Catholic" identity, although they are pressed to say why, having been "soaked in old Catholic marinades, where faith and culture have melded into one" that "seep to the marrowbone."[4]

In the case of Quebec, two dominant forms of ministry seem to be required.

The first is what seemingly is taking place now – service ministry to Catholics who, to borrow and apply the words of an exasperated Toronto Anglican archbishop back in the late 1980s, "are not leaving but are not coming."[5] People engaging in such ministry need to see their work as largely pastoral – providing rites of passage, offering services for those who choose to occasionally attend mass, engaging in counselling, visiting, and other activities expected of a Catholic shepherd.

That said, the survey findings document that some 20% of Quebec Catholics are not closed to greater involvement in parish life. These are people who have been telling us over time that they are looking for vitality in parishes. They are looking for meaningful ministry that is in touch with their interests and needs, along with their family, friends and communities. If they can find it, many indicate that they would consider taking a more active role in parish life.

The Call for Better Ministry across the Nation

In distilling findings from research and conversations spanning approximately four decades now, we have a fairly pointed message for Catholic leaders. To the extent that Catholic women, men and young people can find that faith has a significant impact on their lives, large numbers – even in Quebec – will want to have more to do with the Catholic Church.

But that involvement at this stage in history will not be the result of the Church simply putting expectations on them, so that involvement is essentially "an act of obedience." The day when priests can declare that people should show up for mass every week "because that is what good Catholics do" – the era of what some have referred to as "pray, pay, and obey"[6] – is over.

People, Catholics included, need to find that faith enriches their lives and the lives of those they care about. If not, as we have been emphasizing, most will think, "Why bother?"

That is not to say for a moment that the Church needs to abandon the important message that people who embrace Christian faith are called to commitment, self-denial, discipleship and service. Obviously, those are centrally important components of the Christian life. We are talking here about points of entry – where Canadians, as with the earliest followers of Jesus who were fed, healed and informed, find that their personal needs are being met.

The kind of ministry that touches lives in significant ways, and thereby motivates thousands – even millions – of Catholics to be more involved in the Church and more inclined to live out Christian faith, is also the kind of faith that will continue to be a magnet for Catholic immigrants.

If a Major Goal is Ministry to Immigrants...

New Arrivals

Historically, the Catholic Church has done a very effective job of responding to people who have come to Canada from other places.

The dominant policy seems to have been to allow Catholics to establish new parishes where they could initially live out life in the language and culture of their homeland. Churches thereby retained Catholics in the course of providing them with communities that offered immigrants invaluable social, emotional and spiritual support in their new country.

If second generations wanted to continue to be part of their ethnic parishes, that obviously was possible. However, the existence of English- and French-speaking parishes provided a ready-made network of churches for Catholics who wished to move out of the ethnic settings in which they had been raised. In the language of baseball, it has made for an elaborate and effective farm system.

Moreover, Catholics – as we saw earlier – consciously attempted to welcome newcomers to Canada and help them through their initial period of adjustment. Chaplains at ports of entry, information offices and immigrant aid societies were some of the structures that the Church put in place. Religious orders such as the Oblates made conscious and concerted efforts to minister to newcomers.

Figure 6.1 Religious Identification of Immigrants: 2006-2012 (%)

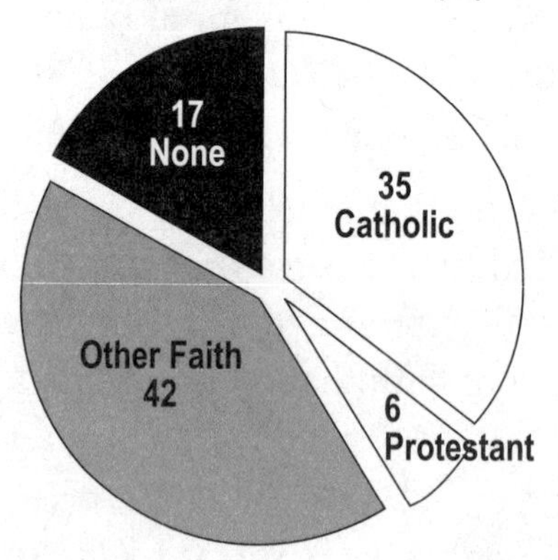

Source: GSS 2012.

Refugees

But it's hardly a matter of the Catholic Church simply responding to people who arrive in Canada by their own choice. The Syrian refugee crisis in late 2015 was a poignant reminder that there are times when the global Church and the Church in Canada need to be alert to the needs of people and to initiate responses. The UN Refugee Agency estimated that, as of mid-September of 2015, more than 4 million people had fled Syria's civil war, with more than 2 million arriving in Turkey.[7]

In response, Pope Francis was direct in calling for parishes, religious orders and other religious institutions to take in refugees. In a radio interview, he had this to say:

> *When I say that a parish should welcome a family, I don't mean that they should go and live in the priest's house, in the rectory, but that each parish community should see if there is a place, a corner in the school which can be turned into a small apartment or, if necessary, that they may rent a small apartment for this family [so that they are] provided with a roof, welcomed and integrated into the community.*[8]

He didn't give himself an exemption: the Vatican itself took in two refugee families.[9] Then again, this was the same Pope who, in December 2013, oversaw the giving of Christmas presents to 2,000 immigrants at a shelter near the Vatican. The packets included a signed Christmas card, postage stamps, a pre-paid international calling card, and a day pass for the Rome metro – things that enabled the people to connect with their families during the festive period.[10]

In Canada, the president of the Canadian Conference of Catholic Bishops, Archbishop Paul-André Durocher, in a widely circulated letter, called on Catholics to respond as well. He laid out specifics as to some of the forms those responses might take. Dioceses soon began to accept the challenge.[11]

The Syrian refugee situation was far from a blip on the Canadian Catholic ministry screen. Work with refugees, for example, has been central to people like Mary Jo Leddy, who has been the highly regarded director of Toronto's Romero House for close to three decades and is a well-known author and former Catholic newspaper editor.

She points out that Romero House "is actually four houses and a store-front center in a little pie-shaped, no-name neighborhood in the west end of Toronto." Each house has political refugees from all over the world, along with some younger interns. "We welcome strangers and live with them as neighbors," she says, "trying to love them as ourselves." Leddy suggests that, "For many of them it is the first time in which they experienced that they would be treated with complete respect, offered affection, regardless of their tribal origin or religious commitment. It is the first time in which someone has given them something – for nothing."[12]

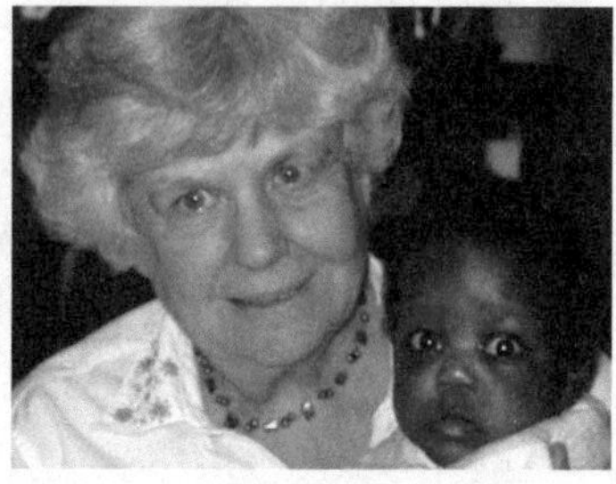

Mary Jo Leddy and friend

Give and Take between Christianity and Culture: Inculturation

With Vatican II, the Catholic church became aware that its evangelization often imposed a foreign culture on people. The church also realized that there is never a cultureless Christianity. Christian faith is always expressed through a particular culture. By the same token, there is never a God-less culture. Every culture has the seeds of faith within it and is capable of bringing its own unique expression to Christianity. At its heart, inculturation means people realizing the Christian Story through their own culture so that they express and live it as their local church and faith. The Church becomes all the more catholic as it encourages diverse expressions of Christian faith through multiple local cultures.

Thomas Groome, *What Makes Us Catholic*, 2003:258-259.

As turbulence continues in various parts of the world, the number of refugees who will need to seek homes in other places – including Canada – will continue. So, presumably, will the expectation of a response on the part of the Vatican.

Table 6.4. World's Top 10 Immigrant Destinations

In Millions as of 2013

10.	Ukraine	5.2
9.	India	5.3
8.	Spain	6.5
7.	**Canada**	**7.3**
6.	France	7.4
5.	United Kingdom	7.8
4.	Saudi Arabia	9.1
3.	Germany	9.9
2.	Russia	11.1
1.	United States	45.8 *

**Includes 12 million Mexicans*

Source: Pew Research Center, September 2, 2014.

With the accelerated wave of immigration on the horizon, it is centrally important for the Catholic Church to continue to be ready and waiting as new people arrive. It is uniquely positioned among Christian bodies, given its global reach and the fact so many of the newcomers will be Catholics.

As we've been emphasizing, what's so important about the immigration wave of the next 50 years – leading up to Canada's 200th anniversary in 2067 – is that immigration is going to be the motor that sustains the nation's population level, in light of the lack of growth through natural increase.

Leaders are well aware that the arrival of large numbers of Catholics raises a number of very important response questions that need to be addressed. Among them are the following:

1. How can the Church help newcomers adjust to Canada?
2. How can parishes provide welcoming environments?
3. To what extent will new parishes be created?
4. What can be done to ensure that the high levels of commitment and involvement that are characteristic of many immigrants continue?
5. What can be done by way of superb family ministry to en-

sure that enthusiasm for the faith continues to characterize *the second generation* of newcomers?

The ongoing influx is a marvellous gift – accompanied by an incredible responsibility.

If a Major Goal is the New Evangelization…

Since the late 1990s, the Catholic Church has given considerable attention to the concept of what it calls "the New Evangelization." In the Church's *General Directory for Catechesis*, released by the Vatican in 1997, normal forms of evangelism were acknowledged as important. But specific attention was also given to Catholic adults "in need of different types of Christian formation" – people in "an intermediate situation":

> *Entire groups of the baptized have lost a living sense of the faith, or even no longer consider themselves members of the Church and live a life far removed from Christ and His Gospel. Such situations require 'a new evangelization'.*

Applied to Canada, this means not being satisfied with having millions of people simply identifying themselves as Catholics, without embracing faith, being involved in parishes or attempting to bring faith to bear on everyday life.

Simply put, the goal is to revitalize millions of nominal Catholics.

That's a mighty tall order, especially in Quebec. So where might the Church begin?

The Sheep Are Already Home

In his important book, *Secularity and the Gospel: Being Missionaries to Our Children*, Ron Rolheiser writes that "We do not know how to get people who are not already going to church to enter those doors."[13] Maybe. But when it comes to wanting to interact with its people, the Catholic Church in Canada has a huge tactical advantage over most other religious groups, including Protestants.

Groups like Anglicans and Baptists and Pentecostals that want to relate to their people have historically used metaphors and models to the effect of having to go out and find them. That's why biblical parables relating to lost sheep, for example, have readily resonated with their plight. For the most part, they have to "go out to the highways and byways" and locate people who have been part of their religious families.

The incentive to do that, however, is neutralized considerably by the fact that most Protestants assume that if a person who "used to be" Anglican or Baptist or Pentecostal is no longer actively involved in a local church, then – for all intents and purposes – they no longer are Anglican or Baptist or Pentecostal. They are pretty much "religious free agents" who are up for grabs.

If all that sounds foreign to a Catholic, it should. You know why. When someone has been baptized as a Catholic, he or she is a Catholic for life. The person might not be involved and might be variously referred to as an ex-Catholic, inactive, non-practising or lapsed. But the individual is still "Catholic."

In Terms of Biblical Metaphors...

MOST OTHER GROUPS
The Lost Sheep Approach

CATHOLICS
The Lost Coin Approach

Of considerable importance, it's not just a matter of the person retaining a Catholic identification. People who think they are Catholic are far more inclined than most other religiously inactive individuals to show up on occasion for services – in large part, it seems, because of a felt need to participate in the Eucharist at least once in a while. Hence, a nominal Catholic can be heard to utter a line that virtually never would come out of a nominal Protestant's mouth: "I feel like I need to go to church next weekend." As the colourful Catholic priest Andrew Greeley – who doubled, no tripled, as a prominent sociologist and bestselling novelist – once put it, "The

Eucharist is a particularly powerful and appealing Catholic ritual, even when it is done badly (as it often is) and especially when it is done well (which it sometimes is)."[14]

For many Protestants – active and otherwise – all that a Communion Sunday (they typically take place only once a month) means is an extra-long service. For Catholics, something special – mystical – is taking place.

Similarly, Catholics feel a need to show up for some special seasonal services, notably Christmas and Easter. Moreover, for large numbers of Catholics, the Church needs to be involved in births and weddings and funerals. Catholic young people have been seen by many as not particularly involved in recent decades. Yet Bibby's Project Teen Canada youth surveys spanning 1987 through 2008 showed little decline in the desire for religious rites of passage, particularly in the case of weddings and funerals.[15] (Table 6.5)

Table 6.5. Desire for Religious Rites of Passage in the Future: Catholic Teens, 1987, 2000, 2008 (%)

"In the future, do you anticipate having any of the following carried out for you by a minister, priest, or some other religious figure?"

% Yes

	1987	2000	2008
Wedding Ceremony	93	94	93
Funeral	95	94	93
Birth-related	96	92	89

Source: Reginald W. Bibby, Project Teen Canada Survey Series.

Canadian Catholic Survey Bytes

Attendance: Monthly, Christmas, Weddings, Funerals by Age

	Monthly* *Or more*	Christmas* Season	Wedding In last year	Funeral In last year
18–34	22%	44%	34%	46%
35–54	15	51	23	58
55+	25	51	18	60

Source: *ARI Christmas 2014 Survey; ARI 2015 Religion Survey.

Catholic Christian Outreach

CCO is a university student movement dedicated to evangelization and leadership formation.

Founded by André and Angèle Regnier at the University of Saskatchewan in 1988, CCO has since grown to serve thousands of students across the country.

Catholic Christian
OUTREACH

Through campus-based outreach, mission projects and national conferences, CCO strives to lead students to encounter Jesus Christ, and enter into a life-changing personal relationship with Jesus and the Catholic Church. In addition, CCO provides multilingual evangelistic materials to parishes and groups worldwide.

CCO is supported through a network of individuals and groups who offer their encouragement, financial sponsorship, and prayers. CCO equips and empowers young leaders to become missionary disciples in their professions, families, and communities.

Source: Catholic Christian Outreach website: www.cco.ca.

Back to "the Catholic advantage": so it is that Catholics are inclined to show up on their own in the course of attending occasional services, attending seasonal services and pursuing valued rites of passage. Parishes do not typically have to engage in major searches. The fact is that many of the sheep are not really all that far from home. Most wander back on their own every once in a while. Protestants have to find them; Catholics just need to tag them! Put less crassly, Catholics need to take note of who these people are.

As if Catholics don't already have a sufficient contact advantage over most other religious groups, let's not overlook still another tremendous advantage: *Catholics also have their schools!* In many parts of the country, Catholic parents have enrolled their children in Catholic schools. As a result, the Catholic Church, through children and teens attending Catholic schools, has links to millions of Catholic families across the country.

We both have had children who have attended Catholic schools. That means our children have also been linked to Catholic parishes and Catholic priests and other parish workers. That link is potentially of incredible importance in the parish being in a position to maximize ministry – not only to young people, but also to their parents and other family members.

And we would rush to offer a simple hypothesis based on our own experiences with Catholic schools: if Catholics can be conscious of that fairly obvious link to families, and the school and parish can work together to elevate life for students and their families, everyone involved will be inclined to want to have more to do with the Church and with Christian faith.

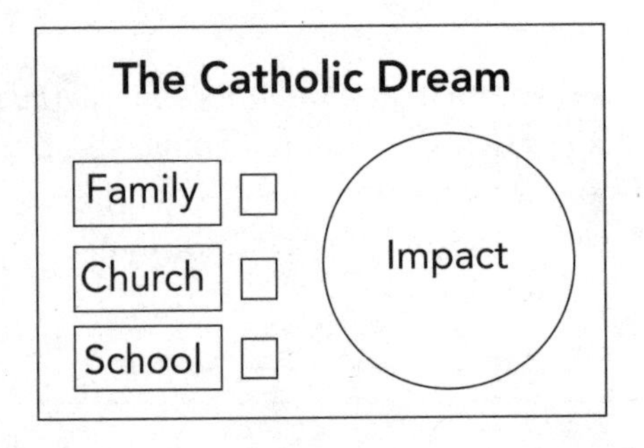

The Prevalence of Catholic Schools

There are approximately 2,000 Catholic schools across Canada, with a total enrollment of more than 800,000 students. Two thirds of the schools are in Ontario. Quebec and the Atlantic provinces do not have what are referred to as "denominational schools."

As of 2015, the number of Catholic schools and their approximate enrollments were as follows:

British Columbia	79	33,000
Alberta	391	158,000
Saskatchewan	119	60,000
Manitoba	17	7,000
Ontario	1,318	546,000
Territories	4	1,600
TOTAL	1,928	805,600

Source: Varied Catholic and other provincial education websites, 2015.

A simple example. There is an old corny line about a sociologist being someone who goes to the hockey game and watches the crowd. As Bibby has stood in Catholic school hallways over the years waiting for the school bell and his daughter, he has become aware that the school has links to many parents who could use some good ministry. Life is good for many moms and dads most of the time. There are lots of laughs and lots of joy. But there also is a lot of strain and pain that calls out for a response – anxiety about health, relationships, money, careers, children – concerns with which all of us are personally familiar. Take note: these people do not have to be located; they are already "there" because of their children.

The Five Essential Marks of Catholic Schools

1. ***Inspired by a Supernatural Vision***: seeks to fix children's eyes on God, on their spiritual dimension
2. ***Founded on a Christian Anthropology***: commitment to the development of the whole person
3. ***Animated by Communion and Community***: faith community, teamwork – school, students, parents, Church
4. ***Curriculum Imbued with a Catholic Worldview***: what is taught is taught through the eyes of Catholic faith
5. ***Sustained by Gospel Witness***: life witness of teachers and administrators who are practising Catholics

Conclusion: schools need to review their effectiveness in realizing these five benchmark indicators of their Catholicity.

Source: Archbishop J. Michael Miller, *The Holy See's Teaching on Catholic Schools,* 2006.

What an opportunity for ministry ... and for evangelism. If the Catholic dream of life-giving "triangular ministry" could take place, where schools increasingly become cultures of caring, working consciously in tandem with parish personnel – principals and priests and other key players – to maximize life-giving responses, some terrific things could take place.

Catholic education as one of the most important challenges for the Church

"Catholic education is one of the most important challenges for the Church," remarked the Holy Father in his address to participants in the plenary session of the Congregation for Catholic Education. Pope Francis proposed three aspects for the participants to consider: the value of dialogue in education, the qualified preparation of formators, and the responsibility of educational institutions to express the living presence of the Gospel in the fields of education, science and culture. Education in our times, he said, "is guided by a changing generation," and every educator and the Church as a whole "is required to change, in the sense of knowing how to communicate with the young."

To borrow the words of Vancouver Archbishop J. Michael Miller, in his presentation "10 Tips for Evangelizing Your Children," given at the World Meeting of Families in Philadelphia in September 2015,

> *My conclusion is that the family, school and parish should increasingly strive together to integrate the ongoing evangelization and catechesis of young people, preparing them for a mature, adult life in the Church. The greater the mutual collaboration and exchange among all those involved in this common endeavor and the more affectionate the relationships among them, the more effective their efforts to educate our young people will be.*[16]

Engaging Them

This takes us back to the "What will it take?" question. Given that inactive Catholics show up on their own, what would make them want to show up more often?

Years of carrying out research on religious involvement and conversations with inactive Catholics and "marginal others" leads us to a rather straightforward conclusion: people give their lives and resources to the kinds of things that they define as significant. If something taking place in parishes resonates with their lives and the lives of the people they care most about, they will want to have more to do with those parishes. It comes back to the highly subjective "worthwhile" issue.

- If people who come to a church for that special seasonal service and unexpectedly discover something meaningful – maybe it's the music or the homily or the Eucharist or the people present – they may find themselves wanting more.
- If people can find that a husband or wife or partner is taken by something that is happening at a service, they may find themselves wanting to support that person and personally explore what is taking place.
- If people can find that their children are not just having to accompany them to church, but actually are enjoying an activity or a group of friends or the music, they may want to ensure that their children continue to be involved.

In short, if being involved in the parish functions to elevate one's life and the lives of loved ones, we believe that people will want to have more to do with the parish. Conversely, if one's attendance and that of family members becomes little more than a ritualistic act, performed out of habit or obedience, little wonder that time-pressed individuals will find better things to do with their weekends. Little wonder that their partners and children will likewise prefer to do other things.

It is virtually an axiomatic conclusion based on our years of research: Catholics and other Canadians are not in the market for churches. Nowhere have we found support for the idea that people are looking for so-called good churches. But they are in the market for good ministry.

If Catholics "have lost a living sense of the faith, or even no longer consider themselves members of the Church and live a life far removed from Christ and His Gospel," but still are walking through church doors, the key to rejuvenation is a rejuvenated Church. They need to be able to find significance in what is taking place: ministry that touches and enriches their lives and the lives of the people they care most about.

The Point of Connection

Key Question:
What is the tangible bridge?

The Answer: **Ministry**

Here we would return to our emphasis on good ministry to families – in the Catholic case, often beginning with children in Catholic schools. Our respective research efforts over the years have led us to conclude that there is nothing more important to Canadians than their families. The policy implication: if we want to have an impact on people's lives, have an impact on their families: their youngest members, their oldest members and those in between. For starters, a good rule of thumb is that every parent wants good things for their children. Do something that elevates life for their kids – including "helping them to turn out all right" – and you will be valued by moms and dads.[17]

And yes, for at least a good number of the 20% or so of Catholics in Quebec who say they are open to greater involvement, we believe those kinds of emphases on ministry to families will be embraced as "worthwhile."

If a Major Goal is Spirituality and Service…

Contrary to playful media descriptions, Pope Francis is not the CEO of the Catholic Church; he is the spiritual leader of the more than one billion people around the world who see themselves as Catholics. In his first Angelus address at the Church of Saint Anne – the parish church in Vatican City – in March 2013, Francis said, "The strongest message of the Lord is mercy." He went on to say,

"Jesus forgets. He has the special capacity to forget. He forgets, he kisses, he embraces, and he only says, 'Neither do I condemn you; go, and from now on sin no more.' The Lord never gets tired of forgiving. Never. We are the ones who get tired of asking him for forgiveness."[18] Canadian journalist and priest Father Raymond de Souza commented, following Pope Francis' U.S. visit in 2015, that his "triumphal tour inspired so many, including those rather distant from the practice of religion, in large part because he so transparently has been transformed by the joy of the Christian gospel."[19]

A Critically Important Asterisk*

Leaders and members are well aware that thousands – no, millions of Catholics – have felt alienated from the Church because they feel their lives are out of sync with Church expectations. They include Catholics who are divorced, are gay, have had an abortion, or perhaps have been abused or have felt abandoned or undervalued by the Church. They include large numbers of women.

It is significant that Pope Francis has consciously been attempting to reach out to such Catholics, calling for mercy and compassion toward people on the margins of the Church. He has been quoted as saying that a Church is needed that will "heal the wounds and warm the hearts of the faithful" and bring "nearness" and "proximity," rather than compounding alienation and exclusion. Tangibly, he has changed annulment procedures, responses to abortion, declared that more influence and authority must be given to women, and shown openness toward people in the LGBT community. He has condemned sexual abuse, and vowed that "all responsible will be held accountable."

As the editor of *The Tablet* has put it, "Francis puts all this in the context of evangelization. He is concerned not just with spreading the Gospel to those who have never heard it. His priority during the Jubilee Year is with bringing back the lost sheep who have been alienated by the way the Church's moral teaching has been presented to them, finding it harsh and unforgiving."

Sources: Bajekal 2015; Hale 2015; *The Tablet*, 2015.

The serene depths of the spirituality of Pope Francis personify the kind of devotion to which Catholics aspire. It is not simply about attendance and participation, or beliefs and practices. It is about being in a deep relationship with God, which in turn has a significant, tangible impact on how one lives life and relates to others. Francis, for example, is said to be "a pope who insists that building a better world begins not with a political platform but with personal conversion."[20]

As readers know well, the Catholic Church has much to offer by way of spiritual expressions that have at their core prayer, meditation, the Scriptures and experiencing God. The Church has a wealth of historical and present-day resources for nurturing spiritual needs.

The Church has not lacked for a large number of religious orders and individuals who express spirituality in diverse ways. Some of the prominent 20th- and 21st-century people who have provided spiritual resources include Thomas Merton, Dorothy Day, Basil Pennington, Henri Nouwen, Jean Vanier, Joan Chittister and Ronald Rolheiser.

A central emphasis is that spirituality should be transformative, in that it affects one's life and, in turn, the lives of others. As such, spirituality and service go hand in hand. In the Pope's words, "Christian truth is attractive and persuasive because it responds to the profound need of human life, proclaiming convincingly that Christ is the Savior of the whole man and of all men."[21] Francis exuded spirituality on his 2015 trip to the United States. But as Michael Higgins points out, "This did not stifle his prophetic inclinations: He championed the cause of refugees and immigrants ... he pushed for the elimination of the death penalty ... he extolled the value of the person in a society of atomized individuals seen primarily as both consumers and commodities."[22]

Collective and Individual Efforts

As we have seen and as most readers know well, the Catholic Church in Canada historically has placed primary emphasis on deep devotion going hand in hand with ministry to the needs of its people and others. Often religious orders have been heavily involved.

- The Church's ministry has been institutionally multi-faceted, taking the tangible form of schools, hospitals, health care, family services, broader social services and a wide range of charities. As with Pope Francis today, the theme of addressing the needs of "the poor and the marginalized" has been central.

- Over time, homes and shelters and hostels have been established for orphans, youth, unmarried mothers and their infants, immigrant women and men, refugees, people with special needs and others requiring care.
- Where such services have not existed, the Catholic Church has had a track record of stepping up to provide them. As governments have expanded their own services, the Church has continued to play a supplementary and complementary role.

So it is that Canada's 61 Catholic dioceses across the country continue to place major emphasis on social ministry. Here are just a handful of examples:

- In Vancouver, Catholic Charities dates back to the "Hungry Thirties" and has provided many social services in Greater Vancouver. Some include a men's hostel, a drop-in centre, prison ministry and refugee sponsorship.[23]
- In Edmonton, Catholic Charities attempts to provide people, "regardless of faith, culture, creed, sexual orientation, or financial status," with the help they need through Catholic Social Services and the Sign of Hope Society. The common goal is "to protect the innocent and empower the weak." More than 60,000 children, women and men receive help each year.[24]
- In Toronto, Catholic Charities collaborates with 26 member agencies in responding to the varied needs of the community, regardless of who they are, serving more than 200,000 people each year.[25]
- In Montreal, Catholic Community Services works with seniors, runs community development programs for youth and operates summer camps for inner-city children. However, in 2015, it dropped the name "Catholic" and became "Collective Community Services." The word "Catholic," said Fred Jansen, the agency's director general, "scares people away – just as the Young Men's Christian Association is now just the 'Y.'"[26]
- In St. John's, various denominations sponsor Emmaus house, which offers food and other services to the poor and needy. The

Society of St. Vincent de Paul has branches in several parishes to provide assistance to people who need food, clothing and shelter. The Sisters of Mercy and Sisters of the Presentation collaborate to provide a drop-in centre for the poor and homeless and offer support for people in need "in rural and outport communities" as well in women's and youth correctional facilities.[27]

Canada's Catholics have been doing – and continue to do – a highly conscious and effective job of ministering to general social needs in their communities and regions.

The Role of Catholic Charities

Many people have asked what the world would look like without the Catholic Church. Well, one obvious difference would be the absence of all the Catholic charity agencies and the wonderful and important work that they do. In many cases, there would be no charity agencies at all, had the Catholic Church not first started doing this work.

How often is it, in so many places in the world, where, after a war, natural catastrophe or social crises, the Catholic Church is the only entity on the ground helping those in need? This may not be as obvious in North America as in developing nations, but the reality is that, even in First World nations, the Catholic Church is the world leader when it comes to providing care for the needy. In Canada, a country known for its vast social services, many of these government agencies would not exist, not even the education system, had the work not been first done by the Catholic Church.

Carlos Ferreira, "A world without Catholic Charities?"
Salt and Light TV Blog, April 12, 2013.

There also have been some notable societal contributions on the part of individual Catholics. The remarkable ministry of Jean Vanier comes to mind.

His story is well known, and details are offered on his personal website.[28] He was born in Canada in 1928. His father was Georges Vanier, Governor General of Canada from 1959 to 1967; his diplomatic career took the family to France and England, where Jean spent his childhood. He earned a doctorate in Philosophy in 1962

from the Catholic University of Paris and taught briefly at St. Michael's College in Toronto. However, in 1964, at the age of 36, he returned to a village near Paris where he previously had assisted in work with men with intellectual disabilities. "There I discovered," writes Vanier, "the plight of men and women who had been put aside, looked down upon, sometimes laughed at or scorned. They were seen as misfits of nature, not as human beings."[29] He soon after was touched by the distressing living conditions of two men, Raphael and Philippe, in a psychiatric hospital. "They never went to school," he recalls, "and when their parents died they were put into this dismal asylum."[30] He decided to buy a small house in a village north of Paris to welcome and live with his two new companions. It was the beginning of a new life that was radically different from anything they had known before, characterized by adjustments and guesswork. He recalls, "Essentially they wanted a friend. They were not very interested in my knowledge or my ability to do things, but rather they needed my heart and my being."

Within a couple of years, other such homes were born, and people from other European countries and Canada responded to Vanier's call for help, becoming assistants who chose to live with people with intellectual disabilities. The communities came to be known as L'Arche – literally, "The Ark" – and today there are some 150 of them spread over five continents, with more than 5,000 members.

Paralleling L'Arche, Vanier co-founded Faith and Light in 1971 with Marie-Hélène Mathieu. These "communities of encounter" are woven around people of all ages living with intellectual disabilities. They, along with their family and friends, participate in monthly meetings during which they share friendship, prayer and celebration. There are some 1,500 Faith and Light communities in 82 countries on five continents.

Jean Vanier has authored some 30 books. The public honours for his lifelong work include his being appointed a Companion of the Order of Canada (1986) and receiving the prestigious Templeton Prize (2015) that acknowledges "an exceptional contribution to affirming life's spiritual dimension."[31]

Although he travels widely, he still lives in the original L'Arche community in France. In a 2008 updated introduction to his Massey lectures of 10 years earlier, Vanier wrote, "We live together – those with disabilities and those who wish to have a deep and sometimes lasting relationship with them. We laugh and cry and sometimes fight with one another; we work, we celebrate life, and we pray together." He adds, "Believe it or not, it has been this life together that has helped me become more human … to recognize and accept my weaknesses and vulnerability. I no longer have to pretend I am strong or clever or better than others. I am like everybody else, with my fragilities and my gifts."[32]

The Coming Boomer Crunch

We have talked a lot about demographics – globalization, immigration and Canada's inability to sustain its population through natural increase in the form of births minus deaths.

But one point we want to underline is the subtext of our emphasis on the importance of people from other countries picking up the population slack from about 2020 onward. That's the fact that, for about two to three decades, or from about 2010 through 2040, the proportion of Canadians age 65 and over is going to jump from a current 15% or so of the population to close to 25%. By around 2050, things will settle down considerably as the Boomers leave the scene. (Figure 6.2)

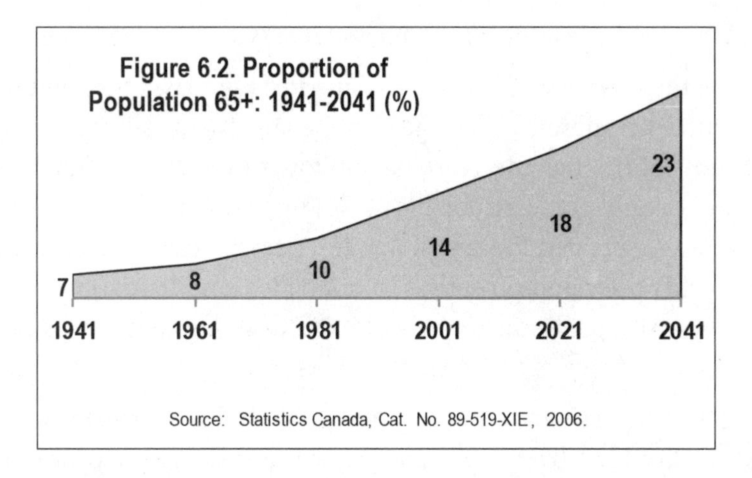

In the meantime, the Catholic Church – like everyone else – is going to be top-heavy with older Canadians, while seeing growing numbers of younger immigrants, led by Asians, also occupying the pews.

From the standpoint of ministry, that means that over the next few decades, the Church has to be prepared not only for a very large influx of young immigrants, but also the presence of a very large number of Canadian-born Catholics who are 65 and older. To be sure, the latter development isn't necessarily the bad news some observers frequently declare it to be. Lots of those older attendees are going to be reasonably affluent people who will bring considerable expertise to parishes, especially with mandatory retirement a thing of the past. On the downside, to be perfectly candid, some won't make it beyond their early 70s, and large numbers who do live longer will increasingly encounter health problems.

Regardless of the various scenarios involved, our point is that the Catholic Church needs to be both well aware of and well prepared for this demographic surge in older people. Depending on the variations, the Church needs to be ready to co-opt their resources as it engages in ministry, as well as refocus its resources and priorities to ensure that it can respond, as needed, to this large cohort of aging Catholic Baby Boomers.[33]

We give the last few thoughts about service to Pope Francis.

On the final day of his visit to Ecuador, Bolivia and Paraguay in July 2015, he offered a message of hope and encouragement to the residents of the Banado Norte shantytown in Paraguay. Some one million people gathered for his closing mass. One media account from the Associated Press said that he "put into practice his call for the world's poor and powerless to not be left on the margins of society by visiting a flood-prone slum and insisting that the Catholic Church be a place of welcome for all – sick and sinners especially."

When he arrived in Banado Norte, he told the cheering crowd that he "couldn't have left Paraguay without being on your land." Francis said he wanted to visit the neighbourhood of plywood shacks and corrugated metal "to see your faces, your children, your elderly, and to hear about your experiences and everything you went through to be here to have a dignified life and a roof over your heads. How much pain can be soothed, how much despair can be allayed in a place where we feel at home." One 82-year-old widow who had lived in the shanty since 1952 commented, "Now I can die peacefully. It's a miracle that a pope has come to this muddy place."[34]

John Allen Jr. has written that "the first thing Francis wants you to know is that Christ came to offer love and salvation to all, but in a special way to the poor." Allen points out that this is not an emphasis that just came to Francis after his election, but reflects his thinking and life over his entire career. "We live in the most unequal part of the world, which has grown the most yet reduced misery the least," he told a gathering of Latin American bishops in 2007. "The unjust distribution of goods persists, creating a situation of social sin that cries out to heaven and limits the possibilities of a fuller life for so many."

But economic poverty is not his only concern. He also has been reaching out to those who know a kind of social poverty and are stigmatized by others.[35] During his U.S. trip in 2015, he exited his car in Philadelphia to kiss the forehead of a boy with cerebral palsy,[36] just as he had embraced a disfigured man at St. Peter's Square some two years before in a scene that went viral on social media.[37]

In November 2013, Francis outlined a new mission statement for the Church that was consistent with his outlook. In his apostolic exhortation *Evangelii Gaudium* (The Joy of the Gospel) he said, "I prefer a church which is bruised, hurting and dirty because it has been out on the streets, rather than a church which is unhealthy from being confined and from clinging to its own security."[38]

The Catholic dream is more than a dream about people being in pews and reciting creeds. It sees people embracing faith, growing spiritually and bringing faith to bear on everyday life.

That kind of Christian maturity involves a lifetime of learning and growth. Here, Canadian parents, the school and the parish work together to plant the seeds and nurture lives. Compassion is taught, encouraged and practised, beginning with babies and with baby steps.

But spiritual growth and service, as we see it, is the heart of Christian faith, and is the ultimate goal for Catholics.

An attainable goal? Yes. Elusive? Yes. Essential to pursue? Yes.

To the extent that the major goals of Catholic leaders are variously greater involvement, ministry to immigrants, the New Evangelization, and spiritual growth and service, it is no mystery how each of those four goals can be achieved.

What is needed now are ongoing tangible responses.

7

Achieving the Possible and the Impossible

These findings from our own surveys and the information provided by many others – including Statistics Canada – add up to a decisive conclusion: the future of Roman Catholicism in Canada is extremely bright.

Catholicism is currently the largest religious group in the country by a wide margin. The overwhelming majority of Canadians who identify with the faith show no inclination to turn elsewhere. Currently and into the foreseeable future, the Catholic ranks will increase significantly as people who are Catholic arrive in increasing numbers from around the world.

What is Realistically Possible

Most of the so-called challenges the Church faces are associated with finding ways of responding to the highly diverse interests and needs of its members, stimulating interest, involvement and commitment, responding well to new arrivals, cultivating spiritual growth and continuing to engage in a wide range of service ministries to Catholics and others.

These are, unquestionably, all major tasks. But they also appear to be tasks that the Catholic Church in Canada, with its national and global human and financial resources, is capable of accomplishing, and indeed has been working hard to accomplish for some time.

Our last sentence needs some elaboration. Something we have not given much attention to is the important issue of resources – human and financial.

Human Resources

Some classic lines from the gospels seem apropos here:

And Jesus went about all the cities and villages, teaching in their synagogues and preaching the gospel of the kingdom, and healing every disease and every infirmity. When he saw the crowds, he had compassion for them, because they were harassed and helpless, like sheep without a shepherd. Then he said to his disciples, "The harvest is plentiful, but the labourers are few…." (Matthew 9:35-38 [RSV])

As the new century began, Bibby did something of an inventory of religious personnel resources in Canada.[1] He attempted to provide some estimates of the number of people identifying with groups, and the number of full-time clergy who were available to minister to them. In short, the data looked like this:

- *Roman Catholics* were relying on some 6,000 churches to minister to almost 13 million people – a church-to-person ratio of 1 to over 2,000.
- The United and Anglican denominations together had more congregations than Catholics – approximately 6,800. The church-to-person ratios for *Mainline Protestants* was in the neighbourhood of one church for every 700 people.
- *Conservative Protestants* had more churches than either the Roman Catholics or Mainline Protestants. Well over 7,000 evangelical congregations had denominational links, and approximately another 2,000 were independents. As a result, the church-to-person ratio was typically considerably lower – about one church for every 200 people. (Table 7.1)

Table 7.1. Number of Churches, Affiliates, Ministers, and Ratios: Select Groups

Religious Group	Approx. No. Churches	No. of Affiliates	Ratio: Churches to Affiliates	Approx. No. Cong. Ministers	Ratio: Ministers to Affiliates
Roman Catholic	**6,000**	**12,900,000**	**1:2150**	**8,000**	**1:1600**
Mainline Protestant	**8,800**	**5,892,000**	**1:670**	**5,250**	**1:1100**
United Church	3,800	2,839,000	1:750	2,000	1:1400
Anglican	3,000	2,036,000	1:700	1,500	1:1300
Lutheran	1,000	607,000	1:700	750	1:800
Presbyterians	1,000	410,000	1:410	1,000	1:400
Conservative Protestant	**9,800**	**2,776,000**	**1:280**	**14,000**	**1:200**
Alliance	380	66,000	1:175	1,050	1:60
Baptists	2,000	729,000	1:360	2,000	1:360
Mennonite	550	191,000	1:345	850	1:225
Pentecostal	2,000	369,000	1:185	3,000	1:120
Non-denominational	2,000	780,000	1:390	3,000	1:260

Source: Derived from Reginald W. Bibby, *Restless Churches*, 2004:135.

What all these data added up to was a situation where *Roman Catholics* had a lot of large parishes. But the personnel – some 6,000 diocesan priests and 3,700 religious order priests, and about 2,300 members of religious orders ("Religious") – had extremely high "case loads." If, say, 8,000 priests were working in parishes, the ratio of priests to people worked out to about one priest for every 1,600 Catholics. If all the Religious were working in parishes (which obviously they are not), the personnel-to-people ratio drops to a mere 1:1250. Incidentally, by way of comparison, in the United States, the Catholic Church used to have one ordained priest for every 800 laypeople; by 2002, the ratio had increased to 1:1400.[2]

This information documented an ongoing reality: *Roman Catholics* have had to rely very heavily on lay involvement in order to have the human resources to carry out effective ministry to their people, as well as minister to others.

The problem that large congregations and limited human resources pose was underlined by some important findings from the Project Canada national surveys in 2000 and 2005. We asked Catholics and other Canadians who were attending services at least once a month (1) how aware religious groups had been of their personal problems over the years, as well as (2) the amount of support the groups had provided. The findings for both years were almost identical; we think they still apply.

Table 7.2. Some Fast Facts on American Catholics and Their Resources

CARA

	1965	1990	2015
CATHOLIC POPULATION	**48.5 million**	**62.4 million**	**81.6 million**
With parish connections	46.3 million	55.7 million	68.1 million
Foreign-born adults	---	5.6 million	22.8 million
CLERGY and RELIGIOUS			
Total priests	58,632	52,124	37,578
Diocesan priests	*35,925*	*34,114*	*25,868*
Parishes	*17,637*	*19,620*	*17,337*
Active diocesan priests per parish	*2.0*	*1.4*	*1.0*
Religious priests	*22,707*	*18,010*	*11,710*
Parishes without a resident priest	*549*	*1,812*	*3,533*
Religious			
Sisters	*179,954*	*102,504*	*48,546*
Brothers	*12,271*	*6,721*	*4,200*
LAY LEADERS			
Permanent deacons	---	9,356	18,082
Lay professional ministers	---	---	23,448
Lay ecclesial ministers, parish ministry	---	21,569	39,651
EDUCATION			
Elementary schools	10,667	7,395	5,302
Secondary schools	1,527	1,324	1,200
Colleges and universities	305	228	226

Source: Center for Applied Research in the Apostolate, 2015.

- Contrary to a stereotypical lament about groups not being willing to be there for people, only 4% reported that groups *failed to give them the support they needed when the groups were aware* of what they were going through.
- Another 53% told us that groups generally were *aware of their problems and came through* with appropriate support. They were led by weekly versus monthly attendees.
- However, what was disturbing to learn was that the remaining 43% said their religious groups *were not aware* of their personal problems – although more than 1 in 3 of these same people said they nonetheless found help from them in dealing with their difficulties. Presumably they found nurture in services, social ties and the like.

But here's the punchline for Catholics: while 67% of *Protestants* said their churches had been aware of their problems, the awareness figure in the case of Catholics was only 43%. This means that close to 6 in 10 Catholics reported that their parishes were unaware of their personal problems, compared to 3 in 10 Protestants. (Table 7.3)

Table 7.3. Role of Religious Groups in Providing Support For Active Affiliates in Times of Need

"Generally speaking, when you have encountered personal problems over the years, have your religious groups been..."

	N	Aware & Supported	Unaware but Supported	Unaware & Not Given	Aware But Not Given	Totals
NATIONALLY	**424**	**53%**	**27%**	**16%**	**4%**	**100%**
Weekly	*311*	*60*	*25*	*11*	*4*	*100*
Monthly	*113*	*32*	*33*	*30*	*5*	*100*
Roman Catholics	**157**	**41**	**27**	**30**	**2**	**100**
Protestants	**187**	**61**	**26**	**7**	**6**	**100**

Source: Bibby, Project Canada 2005.

The Protestant figures show that much more needs to be done; 3 in 10 monthly attenders could translate into 1 million people. But in the case of Catholics, if we have our math straight, some 25% of a total of 13 million attending at least once a month works out to more than 3 million people. If 60% say their parishes have not been aware of their problems over the years, we are talking about close to 2 million Catholics. Not good.

Clearly, if good ministry is going to take place that touches the lives of people who are dealing with serious personal problems, parishes have to find ways of providing opportunities for interaction where personal matters might be able to surface – such as social gatherings and any number of small-group activities. Maybe it is also possible for the parish and Catholic schools to complement each other's efforts in ministering to families.

An extremely important implication here is this: if so many Catholic parishes are unaware of the personal concerns of their people who frequently attend, what are the chances that they will be aware of the needs of relatively inactive affiliates – let alone respond to such needs?

We all know, as Bibby reminded readers in *Restless Churches*,[3] that there are some issues we prefer to keep to ourselves. We also know that many people who face serious problems prefer to turn to family members or friends. That could be one reason why churches often are not aware of difficulties that individuals are encountering.

However, the pronounced Catholic and Protestant differences suggest there is more involved than just issues of privacy and family and friend resources. Groups simply are frequently oblivious to the pressing problems that people sitting in the pews around them are facing.

It's not the way things are supposed to be. In describing a mature and fully developed Christian life, the Catholic Church's *General Directory for Catechesis* maintains, "As the vitality of the human body depends on the proper function of all of its organs, so also the maturation of the Christian life requires that it be cultivated in all its dimensions: knowledge of the faith, liturgical life, moral formation, prayer, belonging to community, missionary spirit."[4] "Belonging to community" does not simply mean worship and learning together: "Apart from its didactic aspect, the Christian group is called to be an experience of community."[5] Moreover, "The parish is called to be a fraternal and welcoming family where Christians become aware of being the people of God."[6] Such ideals are hardly realized when member individuals are oblivious to the pain of one other.

When People No Longer Cry

I once visited a psychiatric hospital that was a kind of warehouse of human misery. Hundreds of children with severe disabilities were lying, neglected, on their cots. There was a deadly silence. Not one of them was crying. When they realize that nobody cares, that nobody will answer them, children no longer cry. It takes too much energy. We cry out only when there is hope that someone may hear us.

Jean Vanier, *Becoming Human*, CBC Massey Lectures, 1998:K97.

If Canada's Catholics are serious about ministering to the needs of one another, solutions have to be found.

But don't underestimate the gods! One of the obvious sources of new leadership for the Catholic Church in Canada lies with immigration. Among those people coming to Canada in increasing numbers from Asia, Africa and Latin America are potential leaders.[7] You have seen the transition first-hand: in the place of an aging European priest is a young and energetic priest from the Philippines or India or Mexico or Africa. John Allen Jr. reminds us that it will be some time before the leadership ranks more accurately reflect the Church's changing demographic composition. The future will not see the South simply replace the North. Rather, leaders and ideas, movements and controversies "will radiate out of multiple centers in both North and South."[8] In Canada, with immigration, that will produce an ever-diverse leadership at many levels, starting with local parishes.

Financial Resources

The word in religious circles is that Catholics in Canada – and the United States, for that matter – are not very good "givers." Is that true?

It is difficult to obtain precise information on Catholic Church finances. For example, in assessing the financing of American religion, sociologists Mark Chaves and Sharon Miller wrote that "financial data have not been reported for the Roman Catholic Church since the early 1930s." Using survey data, Andrew Greeley and others found that giving as a percentage of income decreased between the 1960s and 2000.[9]

An extensive analysis of Statistics Canada data on charitable giving in 1997 by Acadia University sociologist Kurt Bowen found that religiously active Catholics gave far less to their church ($127) than all other religiously active Canadians ($482). In Quebec, the figure was $77, compared to $155 in the rest of Canada.[10]

Data from the Canadian Revenue Agency revealed that, in 2010, Catholics donated an average of $140, Presbyterians $744, Baptists $993, and Pentecostals $1,017.[11]

Statistics Canada, in a 2012 report on charitable giving by Canadians, noted that religious organizations receive the largest share of the total value of charitable donations – some 40%. However, predominantly Catholic Quebec residents donated "smaller amounts

The Need to Stay Close to the People

During his first week in office, Pope Francis said Mass at the Vatican's small parish church of St. Anne's. After Mass, Pope Francis stood outside the church and greeted people as they left, patting

kids on the head and kissing them, shaking hands and exchanging hugs, with a quick word and a smile for everybody. It's a scene that plays out at Catholic parishes all across the world every Sunday, of course, but you rarely get to see a pope doing it. Italian papers immediately dubbed him "the world's parish priest."

Based on what we've seen so far, it seems clear that Francis is determined as much as possible not to lose contact with ordinary folks, not to disconnect him from the ordinary venues where pastors develop a sense of what's on the minds and heart of their people.

To evangelize means meeting people where they are, being able to connect with their doubts and their frustrations. Doing that requires knowing people well, and staying close to them – a good tip not just for a pope, but for anyone who hopes to bring Christ to the world.

John Allen Jr., *10 Things Pope Francis Wants You to Know*, 2013, no. 3.

than residents of other regions." The author of the report commented that research in Europe might be informative: it had found that Catholics living in communities where they were strongly in the majority were less likely than other people to make charitable donations.[12]

Beyond regular financial contributions at the parish level, readers are well aware that Catholics in Canada rely heavily on special donations which, in turn, are frequently associated with special initiatives and special events.

- Annual Archbishop and Bishop dinners are held in many dioceses. For example, the annual dinner in Saskatoon is described by the sponsoring Catholic Foundation as "a gala evening of fine dining and entertainment, as well as a chance to gather with old friends and meet new ones, all while supporting a worthy cause: the needs of our diocesan church."[13] In Ottawa, the Archbishop's Seventh Annual Charity Dinner Fundraising Event in 2014 welcomed some 700 guests.[14]

- In addition, the Archdiocese of Edmonton has what it calls a new "integrated annual appeal" entitled "Together We Serve." It is launched at the beginning of Lent, and has replaced nine special collections that were previously taken up in parishes at various times throughout the year. The funds are used to address a range of needs in Canada and elsewhere. In 2014, the goal was to raise $1.6 million; just over $1.7 million was raised.[15]

Canadian Catholic Survey Bytes

"In the last month, have you donated money to a charity?"

	Attend Services	
	Monthly *Or more*	Less Than Monthly
18–34	79%	31%
35–54	65	42
55+	77	49
Men	77	41
Women	69	43

Source: ARI 2015 Religion Survey.

- Similar appeals are found across the country. They include Vancouver (Project Advance), Calgary (Together in Action), Toronto (ShareLife), Montreal (The Annual Collection), Halifax-Yarmouth (The Archbishop's Appeal), Moncton (The Bishop's Annual Appeal), and St. John's (The Archbishop's Appeal).
- In September of each year, the Canadian Conference of Catholic Bishops makes an appeal for financial assistance to

support its work through what is known as "the Collection for the Needs of the Church in Canada."[16] There also are special humanitarian appeals ("emergency collections") made to parishioners in response to tragic events and other global developments – such as the Nepal earthquakes, the Ebola outbreak, suffering in the Middle East, and typhoons in the Philippines.

Cultural Variations in Giving Patterns: The Filipino Example

When Filipinos first arrive in Canada, they follow the Filipino system of church support in which lower- and middle-income families are expected to contribute only small change. Historically, the Spanish crown gave the land, transported clergy to the Philippines, and supplied them with small stipends. Filipinos built the churches by *corvee* or labour.

Thus, in the Filipino church, a weekly collection was not part of the Sunday Observance, but parishioners were accustomed to paying sole fees for what they asked of the church, such as baptisms, marriages and burials. Upon arriving in Canada, the challenges of finding employment, coupled with the need to send money home to their family, add to the challenges facing newly arrived Filipinos.

Yet after a Filipino family becomes established in Canada, buys a car, owns a house, and adjusts to the higher cost of living, the family learns the Canadian volunteer church system of contributions and donates generously.

Terence J. Fay, *New Faces of Canadian Catholics*, 2009:K1911.

- And, of course, individual parishes as well as a large number of organizations such as the Catholic Women's League engage in a wide range of financial initiatives that often also have social functions. These activities have historically included banquets, dinners, catering, bazaars, bake sales, church teas, craft sales, auctions, bridge tournaments and sports pools, to offer just a short illustrative list.

With due respect to such fundraising strategies, maybe part of the problem with inadequate Catholic giving is that people have not been presented with the ministry possibilities that can take place with appropriate funding. There is a well-worn story about an affluent person dying without leaving anything to his church. When a church official sometime later rallied the courage to ask the man's son why, his son looked puzzled as he responded, "You know, I don't think anyone ever asked him."

Meanwhile, in the United States...

In the United States, one reputable researcher, Christian Smith, reports that "Catholics are the least generous financial givers of all groups of American Christians." He writes that studies consistently show "the vast majority of American Catholics give only a paltry amount of money to the Church and other causes – even after figuring in support for Catholic schools." Smith says that in 1960, Catholics donated an average of 2.2% of their incomes, with that figure dipping to 1% between 1963 and 1983. Today 28% of Catholics give away no money at all, and 81% give less than 2% of their income in voluntary financial giving. He draws attention to the stark implications: "The relative stinginess of American Catholics as a group – despite a very generous minority of Catholic financial givers – means that dioceses, parishes, and other Catholic organizations often do not have the material resources to put in place trained staff in catechesis, faith formation, evangelization, Christian education, and youth and young adult ministry."

Christian Smith, Jonathan Hill and Kari Christoffersen, *Young Catholic America*, 2014:16.

Maybe it's time for Catholics to think bigger. A possible Canadian parable? The case of the Archdiocese of Toronto.

In May 2014, the Archdiocese launched one of the largest Church-based fundraising campaigns in Canadian history. The "Family of Faith" campaign set out to raise $105 million to support the ministry goals and material needs of the diocese, which is comprised of 2 million Catholics and 225 parishes. Cardinal Thomas

Collins summed up things this way: "We are a loving family, but sometimes a family needs food on the table. It needs a roof, it may need a bigger house. That's what we are facing." A pilot program saw 10 hand-picked parishes raise over $7 million, with an additional $16 million raised from several individual donors.[17] As of July 2015, the campaign had topped the $100 million mark.[18]

The Toronto experience has to be incredibly encouraging to Canada's Catholics, providing a poignant illustration of the resources that are potentially available when people come to understand the kinds of ministry that are needed and are possible with the proper resources.

Cardinal Collins has offered this succinct view on financial stewardship: "If we have a proper spirit of gratitude for all that we have received from God, and are resolved to act as responsible trustees of God's gifts, then we will be disposed to contribute financially as members of our Church community." "Deep stewardship," he maintains, "begins with gratitude and ends with responsibility." It encompasses "time, talent, and treasure."[19]

Stewardship research – including two of Bibby's studies in both Canada and the United States[20] – make it clear that people are willing to enthusiastically give money to things that they believe are significant. A major task for Catholic leaders is to demonstrate to Canada's Catholics why some centrally important forms of ministry are needed and, indeed, significant.

Going Beyond the Possible

Canada's Catholics face a marvellous opportunity. We can fairly readily lay out a rational sketch of possible goals. To the extent that adequate resources are in place – both human and financial – Catholics just might achieve what is possible.

But it is also possible to envision a Catholic Church in Canada that can do more – to have an even greater impact on Catholics and Canada.

A Blunt Expression of What Could Happen

A few years ago, a young woman who had been a summer student of Bibby's at a prominent Ontario theological school made an intriguing observation. She was a new convert to Catholicism who had been accustomed to some excellent evangelical church preaching and music, as well as some superb Christian education and youth ministry programs. She told him she had been attending services in a large suburban parish near Toronto with her husband and two young children. She then offered an abrupt but intriguing observation: "The church is packed – and they aren't even doing anything!"

Achieving the Impossible: A Papal Example?

A December 2013 CNN poll found that 88 percent of Americans [gave] the new pope a thumbs-up. Given the notoriously fractious state of the Catholic Church in America, where, under normal circumstances, it would be difficulty to get 88 percent of American Catholics to agree on what day of the week it is, such a result is nothing short of remarkable.

Indeed, if Jorge Mario Bergoglio ever becomes a candidate for sainthood, his ability to unify the chronically divided Catholic Church in the United States might well be considered a contender for his first miracle.

John Allen Jr., *Against the Tide: The Radical Leadership of People Francis*, 2014:37.

Her point was simple: in this particular Catholic setting, it was not at all clear that the parish was actively engaged in effective ministry to children, young adults and others. The services were not characterized by particularly good homilies or music. There wasn't much taking place for kids. There wasn't much evidence of an attempt to create a close-knit, caring community.

She was not dumping on the parish. On the contrary, she was saying that the opportunity was there for this parish to engage in effective ministry. Catholics were showing up in significant numbers. They were receptive. They could benefit so much from ministry that touched their lives and those of their young children. It made her think that something good was beginning to take place by virtue of their being there. But so much more was possible if the parish was "doing something." Beginning to understand Catholicism and its potential to touch lives, she felt that it could – and should – do something.

That's what we have in mind when we speak of Canada's Catholics having the potential to "go beyond the possible." The goals that we have been reflecting on are attainable. But it may well be that, in light of its numbers and potential resources, the Catholic Church in Canada can do so much more.

In short, it will be great if Canada's Catholics will pursue what it possible… and then, having climbed that mountain, set their sights on carrying out the seemingly impossible.

Exploring Religious Affinities

We want to close this section by throwing out an idea. Based on our experiences with Catholics so far, we expect that it will be greeted by a range of responses – from the enthusiastically positive to the passionately negative. From a cold sociological point of view, it is a possibility that needs to be seriously considered because it makes perfect sense.

In an increasingly religiously polarized Canada, where people variously embrace faith, reject faith and take a middle-ground, ambivalent position between the two choices, it seems to us that it is very important for religious groups to find out who their friends are.

"Catholic," by definition, means all-embracing and inclusive. In our contemporary Canada, groups that value Christian faith are wise to share their commonalities, enjoy one another, and work together and share their strengths in the name of optimizing life and optimizing ministry.

As we look at the changing religious landscape in Canada, it's clear that a restructuring of religious groups is taking place. Roman Catholics remain the big player, while the Protestant Mainline

(United, Anglican, Presbyterian and Lutheran churches) is fading numerically. Protestant evangelical groups are vying for second place, bolstered by considerable growth through Pentecostal-oriented immigrants, strong retention of their children, and evangelism.

The time has come, it seems to us, for Catholics and evangelical Protestants, in particular, to take seriously those words of Pope Francis that we cited earlier: "If you are different than me, why don't we talk?"[21] Catholics and evangelicals need to explore their affinities. Explicit efforts to carry out Catholic–Evangelical dialogues have been increasing since Vatican II.[22] That's a good start.

Things Are Not the Way They Used to Be

In 1873, at the New York meeting of the Evangelical Alliance, a delegate from Canada expressed an opinion that almost all others at that international Protestant gathering would have approved: "The most formidable foe of living Christianity among us is not Deism or Atheism, or any form of infidelity, but the nominally Christian Church of Rome." Today in Canada, the Catholic–evangelical situation is, to say the least, on a different footing.

An extensive Angus Reid Poll from 1996 [found that of] Canadians who responded positively to evangelical markers, one-fourth were Roman Catholic. Signs of an altered Canadian landscape for evangelical–Catholic relations extend well beyond polling data. When in 1998 Billy Graham held a preaching campaign in Ottawa, the proportion of Catholic churches among sponsoring congregations was the highest ever in the history of Graham's worldwide ministry.

Mutual antagonism between Roman Catholics and Protestant evangelicals was once an apparently permanent fixture. But that was then. Since 1960 a new age has dawned.

Mark A. Noll and Carolyn Nystrom, *Is the Reformation Over?* 2005. K:83, 138, 484.

But much more is necessary – and possible. Reg grew up in Evangelical circles and knows that world well. Since about 2006, he has been exposed to Catholic schools through his daughter's enrollment from pre-school through junior high. He has had his eyes opened to a simple reality: when it comes to Catholic schools, most evangelicals don't have a clue what goes on in there. He has enjoyed having the opportunity to tell Catholic educators across the country that it is time for them to have far more open houses – not only for Catholics, but for Protestants, especially evangelicals. A cursory glance at bulletin boards and hallway art and signs on classroom doors would shock many of them, he says. The schools looks so... well, so evangelical!

The words posted in a Catholic school hallway.

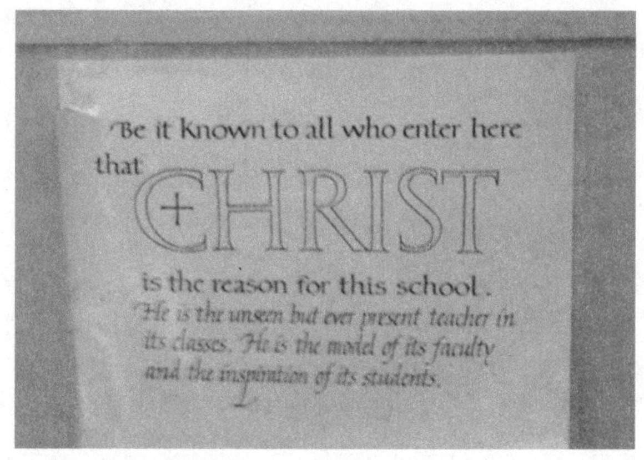

Posted on a Catholic school room door.

Our point is that Catholics and many Protestants have more in common than they realize – and it's high time they discovered it. In a religiously polarized Canada, those who value faith need to explore their commonalities and see what they can accomplish together. No, we are not so naïve as to think such interaction will always result in happy endings. But we think it frequently will… if people will suggest to one another, "Why don't we talk?"

Significantly, research and personal experience tell us that Catholics who are open to closer cooperation with evangelicals have had positive personal connections with evangelicals whose faith they respect. Similarly, evangelicals open to closer cooperation with Catholics have typically had positive personal experiences with individual Catholics who clearly place importance on Christian faith.

Theological specifics don't turn out to matter all that much. As Noll and Nystrom point out, "Differences on basic Christian convictions between Catholics and evangelicals fade away as if to nothing when compared to secular affirmations about the nature of humanity and the world."[23]

Here's to many more conversations.

Conclusion

Beyond Vitality, Hope and Perplexity

As we began work on the pivotal 2015 survey that would provide the heart of the information for this book, we did so believing that we could provide an important update on Catholicism in Canada. We anticipated doing what we both have done throughout our careers – polling Catholics and other Canadians and then proceeding, like the objective sports announcer in the booth, to call things as they are.

While we both value faith, we had no illusions about what we would find. If anything, the dominant thinking of social scientists – including Bibby and Reid – led us to expect that we would probably be documenting, at best, the fact that things were levelling off a bit for Canadian Catholicism as a whole, while still looking fairly bleak in Quebec.

Our Surprising Findings on Vitality and Hope

What we have found as we've looked at our data and put the findings in a global perspective is that Catholicism is experiencing considerable vitality at this point in history. Many observers see its global growth as unprecedented. In addition to the vitality, there is also the totally unanticipated "Francis factor." If some readers have felt that we have given him too much attention, they need to know that, at the outset, we had no such intention. But as we began placing our findings in the broader context of Catholicism worldwide, the emerging impact of Pope Francis – from his appointment in March 2013 through his trip to the United States in September 2015 – only kept accelerating. His American visit provided the Vatican with phenomenal global media exposure. Thanks to the nature of Pope Francis, it is an understatement to say that the exposure was highly favourable to the Catholic Church.

This is a leader who, through at least the first years of his papacy, has been shaking up not only Catholics but very large numbers of people more generally. He has not been without his detractors. But he clearly has had a profound effect on the global perception of the emerging Catholic Church. A year into his papacy, he was described by one prominent American writer as one whose image projects "a kinder, gentler Catholicism" that has "inspired many of the lapsed, the recovering, the former and the fallen to reconsider the possibilities of being Catholic without qualification."[1] As one *New York Times* journalist has put it, "Francis has changed its emphasis, projecting a merciful, welcoming tone in a church that had been shattered by clerical sexual abuse scandals and identified with theological rigidity."[2] An array of poignant lines on his U.S. trip – such as "legislative activity is always based on care for the people," the poor have "sacred rights to labour, land and lodging," "thirst for power and material prosperity leads both to the misuse of available resources and to the exclusion of the weak and disadvantaged," and the powerful, succinct statement that when a child is sexually abused, "God weeps" – only added to the high level of rapport that Pope Francis appears to have with people in the U.S., in Canada and around the world.[3]

Indicative of what seemed to be a prevalent mood, captions displayed on signs, buttons, T-shirts and ball caps during his 2015 U.S. visit involved variations of "The Pope and Hope" theme. Michael Swan of *The Catholic Register* wrote, "It's more than another assignment. There's something in Francis we need to see, to capture, and to know."[4] Illustrative of the hope emphasis associated with him was his plea in the first-ever papal address to Congress for a united response to widespread hatred and violence in the form of "hope and healing, of peace and justice."[5] After he had departed, CNN, for example, reported that "Pope Francis has returned to Rome, leaving the United States with 'a heart full of gratitude and hope.'"[6]

Here again, the take of prominent Vatican-watcher John Allen Jr. seems apt. "People around the world have been charmed, and Catholics in particular sense a new wind blowing in the Church they love. As more than one commentator has observed, in the Francis era, it's 'cool to be Catholic' again."[7] He reminds us that, before Pope Francis, storylines in the global media about the Church tended to focus on sexual abuse by clergy, crackdowns on American nuns, and assorted Vatican scandals. "While those stories have not gone away, today the dominant narrative about Catholicism has become, 'People's pope takes the world by storm!'"[8]

Allen offers a further important observation: "The highest priority of the Catholic Church is supposed to be the New Evangelization, an effort to induce an often jaded world to take a new look at the faith. By any objective measure Francis represents the most attractive missionary calling card that Catholicism has had in quite some time." His charisma "seems to be revitalizing Catholicism and offering it a new lease on life."[9]

Our survey findings, in tandem with "the Francis effect," lead us to a strong sense that the Catholic Church in Canada today exists at a time that is characterized by considerable vitality and hope. Needless to say, such a context is dramatically different from what people who valued faith were experiencing as the 20th century came to a close. It's a new day, to put it mildly.

What is of critical importance is the response to the times. As we have been emphasizing throughout the book, the Catholic Church is Canada's "big religious player." As the Catholic Church goes, so go religious trends in Canada. With its national-leading numbers comes the tremendous challenge to lead the nation. It is in a position, nationally and parish-by-parish, to have a profound impact on both religion in this country and Canadian life as a whole.

Our Perplexing Findings on Diversity and Durability

Throughout our documentation and discussion of the Catholic situation in Canada, we have been giving considerable attention to what, on the surface at least, appear to be at least *two anomalous findings*.

The first is that *Catholics are anything but a homogenous group*, especially when we take into account the Quebec expression of the faith. Beliefs, practices, attendance and parish involvement seem to be all over the proverbial map. Attitudes and behaviour, with respect to sexuality in particular, frequently diverge from the official teachings of the Church.

This common lack of conformity leads us to the second anomalous finding: *Catholics, despite their pronounced heterogeneity, show an incredible inclination to continue to value being Catholic.*

In the face of expectations that (1) their differences will result in their abandoning the faith or (2) their lack of involvement means that they are no longer Catholic, they go on embracing Catholicism.

These two realities, as we have been acknowledging, have led to no little confusion on the part of observers who have been trying to make sense of Catholicism, especially in the context of secularization. People assume that Catholics are turning their back on the Church because they are rejecting teachings and/or not showing up all that much. They are wrong on both counts.

The holding power of Catholicism is nothing short of astounding. Catholics go on thinking they are Catholics.

This brings us back to a central question: what do Catholic leaders want to do about it all?

Do they want Catholics to be more unified in the endorsement of beliefs and practices? Do they want them to be more involved? Is the goal evangelization … or greater service?

If these are some of the primary goals, as we have been emphasizing, there are some tangible steps that leaders might consider taking to see them realized. Those steps are centred on more effective ministry that engages Catholics and makes greater involvement and greater commitment worthwhile and meaningful, elevating their lives and their inclination to want to elevate the lives of others.

But what everyone on the inside and outside of the Church needs to clearly understand is that, diversity and limited involvement notwithstanding, the vast majority of Catholics continue to be Catholic.

Such a reality means that some people will decry individuals and groups that do not conform to their definitions of what "a good Catholic" looks like. One only has to think of people who maintain they are Catholic but take variant positions on issues such as divorce or cohabitation, priests marrying or women's ordination, gay relationships and gay parenthood, contraception or legal abortion. Catholics who are not involved in their parishes are derisively labelled "inactive" or "lapsed." In July 2013, the Archdiocese of Detroit published a warning against some dozen churches in its jurisdiction that it claimed "use the name Catholic but aren't."[10]

To the onlooker, given the array of ideas and participation levels of Catholics, the only thing they seem to have in common is the name. But the fact that, in a country like Canada, such diverse people continue to identify with that name signals the fact that Catholicism – however understood and however practised – remains important to "Catholics" and will continue to remain important in the foreseeable future.

Readers may recall that when Pope Francis was asked in July 2013 about homosexuality, he offered a response that one prominent Vatican observer claims was the most-quoted line uttered by any public figure in 2013:[11] "Who am I to judge them if they're seeking the Lord in good faith?"[12] His words triggered predictably diverse reactions from a highly diverse Church. Martin Marty, the esteemed University of Chicago historian, recently summed things up this way: "There are very many kinds of Roman Catholics today." It was once said, he writes, that Rome "is always the same." But in many ways, even its sameness "is subject to change, and has been from 'Peter' until now."[13] Catholicism – diverse, alive, in constant flux.

John Allen reminds us that the inclination of Catholics to hold widely differing opinions extends to the highest levels of the Church and includes its 5,000 bishops across the world. Further, "among the rank and file, there's pretty much every opinion under the sun. Suffice it to say whatever perspective or point of view you're looking for, you can almost always find it somewhere on the Catholic landscape." How common is debate over beliefs? Allen writes that "Doctrinal debate is almost as common in the Catholic Church as the daily mass." He underlines a central issue: an age-old point of tension that continues today "is how much agreement with official teaching is enough to qualify one as still part of the team – and, of course, who gets to decide."[14]

Final Thoughts: Greeley and Great Potential

So there we have it. Canada's Catholics are living at a time that is characterized by vitality and hope, complete with lots of responsibility for responding to it all. They face the possibility of playing a pivotal role in elevating life for Canadians and the country as a whole.

Theologically speaking – and remember that we are mortal sociologists who have no business doing any excessive pontificating – God, we suspect, expects the Church to respond!

But can God use such a diverse collection of Canadian Catholics to have such an impact? With no sacrilege intended, we would simply defer the call and proclaim that "God only knows."

One of the most influential Catholic sociologists and priests of the last century was Andrew Greeley, who was based in Chicago. He was both a loyal supporter and a fierce critic of the Church. For reasons neither of us can quite comprehend, we never met him. But we read his sociological works and smiled as this prolific researcher, columnist and homily writer expanded his writings to include over 50 novels – and many bestsellers at that. In a 1992 interview with the Chicago *Tribune*, Greeley said, "I'm a priest, pure and simple. The other things I do – sociological research, my newspaper columns, the novels I write

– are just my way of being a priest. I decided I wanted to be one when I was a kid growing up on the West Side. I've never wavered or wanted to be anything but."[15]

In 1994, Greeley wrote an article for *The New York Times* entitled "Why Do Catholics Stay in the Church?"[16] He recalled how, on one occasion, someone asked him why, if he was so critical of Catholicism, he didn't resign from the priesthood and leave the Church. His response? "Why should I leave? I like being Catholic and I like being a priest." Greeley explains in some detail that "Catholics remain Catholic because of the Catholic religious sensibility, metaphors that explain what human life means, with deep and powerful appeal to the total person." He goes on to say that, despite incompetence and moral failings, the hierarchy and clergy have not succeeded in driving lay folk out of the Church "because the lay folk like being Catholic."

And why? Because Catholicism is experience, image and story, and "Catholics like their heritage because it has great stories." They include "stories about angels and saints and souls in purgatory and Mary the Mother of Jesus and stained-glass windows and statues and stations of the cross and rosaries" – as well as "ceremonies that mark the passing of the year – Midnight Mass, the Easter Vigil, First Communion, May Crowning, Lent, Advent, grammar-school graduation and the festivals of the saints." He also goes on to talk about the sacraments, the neighbourhood parish, the Christmas crib, the lady holding Jesus. His summation: "the religious images of Catholicism are acquired early in life and are tenacious. You may break with the institution, you may reject the propositions, but you cannot escape the images."

Greeley concludes the article by recalling an old story that the nuns used to tell that, he says, "sums up why people stay Catholic." Jesus is touring the heavenly city and notes that some new residents shouldn't be there. He storms out to the gate where Peter is checking the day's intake.

"You've failed again, Peter," says the Lord.

"What have I done now?" Peter responds.

"You let a lot of people in who don't belong."

"I didn't do it," Peter protests.

"Well, who did?" asks Jesus.

"You won't like it," replies Peter.

"Tell me anyway," Jesus says.

Then comes Peter's response: "I turn them away from the front gate and then they go around to the back door… and your mother lets them in."

Canada's Catholics are a diverse bunch, but they are also a tenacious bunch, and relatively few are about to leave – even if they have to come in through the back door. These days the Church is experiencing new vitality and new hope. The potential exists for significant things to happen.

What remains to be seen is how Catholics will respond.

Notes

Chapter 1

1 "A Memorable and Prophetical 400th Anniversary." Website of the Catholic Church of Montreal. http://diocesemontreal.org/en/news/latest-news---en/reader/items/a-memorable-and-prophetic-400th-anniversary.html.

2 "History of the Church in Canada." Website of the Canadian Conference of Catholic Bishops. http://www.cccb.ca/site/eng/church-in-canada-and-world/catholic-church-in-canada/history-of-the-church-in-canada.

3 Canadian Heritage website, Government of Canada. http://www.pch.gc.ca/eng/1363629314164/363629390521.

4 Catholic Health Alliance of Canada 2015.

5 Huel 1983.

6 See, for example, Rioux 1978:19, 220–221 and Falardeau 1976:111.

7 Mol 1985:199.

8 "The Rich Diversity of the Church in Canada." http://www.cccb.ca/site/eng/church-in-canada-and-world/catholic-church-in-canada/history-of-the-church-in-canada.

9 Twain 1881.

10 Cited in the CBC Documentary "The Quieter Revolution," 1973.

11 Cited in Bibby 2002a:15.

12 Baum 2000:150.

13 Mol 1985:198.

14 Mol 1985:209–210.

15 Grant 1998:227.

16 Yakabuski 2009.

17 For details and interpretations of the Church's relinquishing its institutional dominance, see, for example, Rouleau 1977, Seljak 1995 and 2000, and Baum 2000:149–158.

18 Bélanger 2000.

19 Baum 2000:151.

20 Cited in Grant 1998:228.

21 Seljak 2000:133.

22 Bibby 1993:76–77.

23 For a delineation of that role in light of the Dumont Report (1971), see, for example, Baum 2000:157ff.

24 Bibby 1987:144.

25 Revised slightly upward from 32% estimate in Bibby 2011:37; difference due to "past 7 days" vs. "how often" indicator being used for 1997 to make it consistent with 1957 measure.

26 Grant 1998:228.

Chapter 2

1 See, for example, D'Antonio, Dillon, and Gautier 2013.

2 Some leading contemporary secularization proponents include Bruce 2002 and 2011, and Brown 2009.

3 For an important exposition of these three – individual, institutional and organizational components of secularization – see Dobbelaere 2002; also helpful is Casanova 2006.

4 Allen 2013a:K196.

5 Allen 2009:1, 14.

6 Computed from the 2011 General Social Survey.

7 D'Antonio, Dillon, and Gautier 2013:K623.

8 D'Antonio, Dillon, and Gautier 2013:K623.

9 Pew Research Center, September 2014.

10 Computed from Reginald W. Bibby, Project Canada 2005.

11 Bibby 2012b:16.

12 Fay 2009:K76.

13 Longhurst 2012.

14 Longhurst 2012.

15 Allen 2013a:K98.

16 Allen 2013a:K196.

Chapter 3

1 Graham 1990:121.

2 Collins 2013:K829.

3 Stark and Glock 1968.

4 Betty 2010.

5 Taylor 2007:513.

6 D'Antonio, Dillon, and Gautier 2013:K208.

7 D'Antonio, Dillon, and Gautier 2013:K893ff.

8 They might include such publications as the *BC Catholic*, *Western Catholic Reporter*, *Prairie Messenger* and *National Catholic Reporter*, to name a few. For interesting takes on Catholic journalism, see Sinasac 2015 and Argan 2015.

9 Yakabuski 2009.

10 Groome 2003:164.

Chapter 4

1 Baum 2005:133.

2 Winfield and Rodriguez 2015.

3 See, for example, Regenstreif 1964, McDonald 1969, Irvine 1974, and Engelmann and Schwartz 1975.

4 For expositions of such thinking more generally, see Glock and Stark 1965.

5 See, for example, Lenski 1963, Yinger 1971, and D'Antonio, Dillon, and Gautier 2013:K2082.

6 See, as an example, Janda 1980.

7 For reflections on the extent to which Canadians routinely draw on a variety of "non-empirical" sources in anticipating their futures, see Bibby 2016.

8 Groome 2003:5.

Chapter 5

1 See, for example, Fay 2009.

2 Interview on "As It Happens" with Reginald Bibby, May 4, 1976. Archived on www.reginaldbibby.com.

3 Pew Research Center, April 2, 2015.

Chapter 6

1 The three response options were "Yes," "Perhaps," and "No." Adjusting to include missing values – since some Catholics who were infrequent attenders didn't offer a response – the "Yes" and "Perhaps" totals were 50% in 1995, 52% in 2000, and 60% in 2005.

2 Bibby 2012.

3 Yakabuski 2009. Updated in 2012.

4 Groome 2003:xiii.

5 Garnsworthy 1986.

6 See, for example, D'Antonio, Dillon, and Gautier 2013:K145.

7 Source: UN Refugee Agency website: http://data.unhcr.org/syrianrefugees/regional.php#ga=1.221098072. 1934137780. 1442730451.

8 Interview with Portuguese radio; cited in Kozlowska 2015.

9 See, for example, CNN 2015 and Glatz, Catholic News Service, September 18, 2015.

10 *The Daily Mail Online*, December 20, 2013.

11 See, for example, Ottawa in Gyapong 2015, Toronto in Friesen 2015.

12 Leddy in Rolheiser 2006:136, 138.

13 Rolheiser 2006:16.

14 Greeley 1994.

15 See, for example, Bibby 2009:182.

16 Miller 2015.

17 The antithesis of this positive ministry to children, of course, is child abuse. For an excellent exposition of its nature, sources, consequences, and required responses, see Higgins and Kavanagh 2010.

18 Cited in Allen 2013b:K149, 155.

19 De Souza, September 28, 2015.

20 Allen 2013b:K248.

21 Cited by Allen 2013b:K278.

22 Higgins 2015.

23 Source: http://rcav.org/catholic-charities.

24 Source: http://www.catholiccharities.ab.ca/CatholicCharity/default.aspx.

25 Source: www.catholiccharitiestor.org.

26 Hustak 2015.

27 http://rcsj.org/service-and-outreach.

28 See his personal website for biographical details: http://jean-vanier.org/en/the_man/biography.

29 Vanier 2010:K23.

30 Vanier 2010:K23.

31 https://www.templeton.org/signature-programs/templeton-prize.

32 Vanier 2010: Introduction, K23.

33 For a detailed exposition of Canada's Baby Boomers, see Bibby 2006.

34 Winfield and Rodriguez 2015.

35 Allen 2013b:K66, 72.

36 U.S. News and World Report, September 26. For both chance and planned encounters the Pope had with people with disabilities during his trip, see, for example, Jensen 2015.

37 Karimi 2013.

38 Allen 2014:8.

Chapter 7

1 Much of the material that follows on human resources is drawn from Bibby 2004:134–138.

2 Smith, Hill, and Christoffersen, 2014:15.

3 Bibby 2004:95–96.

4 *General Directory for Catechesis,* 1997:87.

5 *General Directory for Catechesis,* 159.

6 *General Directory for Catechesis,* 257.

7 See, for example, Gonzales 2015 for the story of Fr. Anthony Cruz who has come from India.

8 Allen 2009:15.

9 Chaves and Miller 1999:14.

10 Bowen 2004:27.

11 Phan, 2012.

12 Turcotte 2012:10–11.

13 The Catholic Foundation newsletter, Roman Catholic Diocese of Saskatoon, February 2014:6.

14 Archdiocese of Ottawa Press Release, October 21, 2014. http://catholicottawa.ca/documents/2014/10/Archbishop_Prendergast_hosts_charity_dinner_2014-4.pdf.

15 Archdiocese of Edmonton website, "Together We Serve." http://www.caedm.ca/WeServe.aspx.

16 CCCB website, "2014 Collection for the Needs of the Church in Canada." http://www.cccb.ca/site/eng/members/annual-collection.

17 *Catholic Register*, May 14, 2014.

18 Boudreau, July 2, 2015.

19 Collins 2013:K1006.

20 Bibby 1994 and 2002b.

21 Winfield and Rodriguez, 2015.

22 For a succinct summary of some of the Catholic-initiated ecumenical dialogues since Vatican II, see Noll and Nystrom 2005:K2544ff.

23 Noll and Nystrom 2005:K5342, 5359.

Conclusion

1 Manseau 2014.

2 Yardley 2015.

3 Summarized in Brumfield 2015.

4 Swan 2015.

5 Epatko 2015.

6 Brumfield 2015.

7 Allen 2014:8.

8 Allen 2014:63.

9 Allen 2014:41, 63.

10 Manseau 2014.

11 Allen 2014:6.

12 Allen 2013c.

13 Marty 2014.

14 Allen 2013a:K172, K630.

15 Jensen and Ramirez 2013.

16 Greeley 1994.

References

Agren, David. 2014. "Pope urges U.S. Catholics to keep enthusiasm, welcome newcomers." Catholic News Service. Appeared in *Prairie Messenger*, September 30. http://www.prairiemessenger.ca/15_09_30/pope_15_09_30_17.html.

Allen, John L. Jr. 2009. *The Future Church: How Ten Trends Are Revolutionizing the Catholic Church*. New York: Doubleday.

———. 2013a. *The Catholic Church: What Everyone Needs to Know*. New York: Oxford University Press.

———. 2013b. *10 Things Pope Francis Wants You to Know*. Liguori, MO: Liguori Publications.

———. 2013c. "Pope on homosexuals: 'Who am I to judge?'" *National Catholic Reporter*, July 29. http://ncronline.org/blogs/ncr-today/pope-homosexuals-who-am-i-judge.

———. 2014. *Against the Tide: The Radical Leadership of Pope Francis*. Liguori, MO: Liguori Publications.

Angus Reid Institute. 2013. "Canadian and American Catholics call for a more liberal pope." March 11. http://angusreid.org/canadian-and-american-catholics-call-for-a-more-liberal-pope.

Argan, Glen. 2015. "Editor's grandiose designs had to meet the real world." *Western Catholic Reporter*, September 28. http://www.wcr.ab.ca/ThisWeek/Stories/tabid/61/entryid/6901/Default.aspx.

Bajekal, Naina. 2015. "Pope Francis says Church must listen to women." *Time*, April 15. http://time.com/3822482/pope-francis-women-church-society.

Baum, Gregory. 2000. "Catholicism and Secularization in Quebec." In David Lyon and Marguerite Van Die (eds.). *Rethinking Church, State and Modernity*. Toronto: University of Toronto Press. Pp. 149–165.

———. 2005. *Amazing Church: A Catholic Theologian Remembers a Half-Century of Change*. Ottawa: Novalis.

Bélanger, Claude. 2000. "The Roman Catholic Church and Quebec." *Quebec History*. Montreal: Marianopolis College. http://faculty.marianopolis.edu/c.belanger/quebechistory/readings/church.htm.

Betty, Stafford. 2010. "Why do so many Catholics believe in reincarnation?" Reprinted in *Hinduism Today*. http://www.hinduismtoday.com/blogs-news/hindu-press-international/-why-do-so-many-Catholics-believe-in-reincarnation-/10313.html.

Beyer, Peter. 1993. "Roman Catholicism in Contemporary Quebec." In W.E. Hewitt (ed.). *The Sociology of Religion: A Canadian Focus*. Pp. 133–156.

———. 1997. "Religious vitality in Canada: The complementarity of religious market and secularization perspectives." *Journal for the Scientific Study of Religion*, 36:272–288.

———. 2006. *Religions in Global Society*. New York: Routledge.

Bibby, Reginald W. 1987. *Fragmented Gods: The Poverty and Potential of Religion in Canada*. Toronto: Irwin.

———. 1990. *Mosaic Madness: Pluralism Without a Cause*. Toronto: Stoddart.

———. 1993. *Unknown Gods: The Ongoing Story of Religion in Canada*. Toronto: Stoddart.

———. 1994. *Unitrends. A study report prepared for The United Church of Canada*. Toronto: United Church Stewardship Department.

———. 2002a. *Restless Gods: The Renaissance of Religion in Canada*. Toronto: Stoddart. Paperback edition released by Novalis (Ottawa) in 2004.

———. 2002b. *FutureTrends 2002. A study report prepared for The Cumberland Presbyterian Church*. Memphis: Cumberland Presbyterian Church.

———. 2004. *Restless Churches: How Canada's Churches Can Contribute to the Emerging Religious Renaissance*. Ottawa: Novalis & Kelowna: Wood Lake Books.

———. 2006. *The Boomer Factor: What Canada's Most Famous Generation is Leaving Behind*. Toronto: Bastian Books.

———. 2009. *The Emerging Millennials: How Canada's Newest Generation is Responding to Change & Choice*. Lethbridge: Project Canada Books.

———. 2011. *Beyond the Gods & Back: The Demise and Rise of Religion in Canada*. Lethbridge: Project Canada Books.

———. 2012a. *A New Day*. Lethbridge: Project Canada Books.

———. 2012b. "Why bother with organized religion?" *Canadian Review of Sociology* 49:1, 91–101.

———. 2016. "The future of an allusion: Using social and personal forecasts to uncover explicit and implicit religion." *Implicit Religion* 19.1. In press.

——— and Angus Reid. 2013. "We'll be home for 'Christmas,' however it's celebrated." Commentary, *Globe and Mail*, December 24.http://www.theglobeandmail.com/globe-debate/well-be-home-for-christmas-however-its-celebrated/article16075404.

———, Terri-Lynn Fox, and James Penner. 2010. *Canada's Emerging Aboriginal Millennials: A National Survey Reading of Aboriginal Teens & Other Teens.* Lethbridge: Project Canada Books.

Boguslawski, Steven and Ralph Martin (eds.). 2008. *The New Evangelization: Overcoming the Obstacles.* New York: Paulist Press.

Boudreau, Evan. 2015. "Family of Faith tops the $100 million mark." *The Catholic Register*, July 2. http://www.catholicregister.org/item/20515-family-of-faith-tops-the-100-million-mark.

Bowen, Kurt. 2004. *Christians in a Secular World: The Canadian Experience.* Montreal: McGill-Queen's University Press.

Bramadat, Paul and David Seljak (eds.). 2008. *Christianity and Ethnicity in Canada.* Toronto: University of Toronto Press.

Brierley, Peter. 2006. *Pulling out of the Nosedive: A Contemporary Picture of Churchgoing.* London: Christian Outreach.

Brown, Callum. 2009. *The Death of Christian Britain.* Second edition. London: Routledge.

Bruce, Steve. 2002. *God Is Dead: Secularization in the West.* Oxford: Blackwell.

———. 2011. *Secularization: In Defense of an Unfashionable Theory.* Oxford: Oxford University Press.

Brumfield, Ben. 2015. "Pope Francis surprised by warmth of Americans and devoutness of the faithful." CNN, September 28. http://www.cnn.com/2015/09/28/us/pope-trip-wrap-vatican.

Canadian Conference of Catholic Bishops. 1992. *From Pain to Hope: Report from the CCCB Ad Hoc Committee on Child Sexual Abuse.* June. http://www.cccb.ca/site/Files/From_Pain_To_Hope.pdf.

Canadian Conference of Catholic Bishops. 2015. "The Catholic Church in Canada and Indigenous Peoples." http://www.cccb.ca/site/eng/church-in-canada-and-world/catholic-church-in-canada/indigenous-peoples.

CanadaVisa.com. 2015. "Atlantic Canada: An increasingly important immigration destination." http://www.canadavisa.com/atlantic-canada-important-immigration-destination.html.

Casanova, José. 2006. "Rethinking secularization: A global comparative perspective." *The Hedgehog Review*, Spring & Summer.

Catholic Health Alliance of Canada. 2015. *The Great Canadian Catholic Hospital History Project.* http://www.chac.ca/about/historyproject_e.php.

Catholic Register. 2014. "Archdiocese of Toronto launches $105 million campaign." May 14. http://www.catholicregister.org/item/18157-archdiocese-of-toronto-launches-105-million-campaign.

Catholic World Report. 2014. "Pope Francis offers three proposals for improving Catholic education." February 13. http://www.catholicworldreport.com/Blog/2929/pope_francis_offers_three_proposals_for_improving_catholic_education.aspx#.Uv2Hvvco7IU.

Center for Applied Research in the Apostolate. 2015. "Frequently requested Church statistics." http://cara.georgetown.edu/frequently-requested-church-statistics.

Chaves, Mark. 2011. *American Religion: Contemporary Trends*. Princeton, NJ: Princeton University Press.

——— and Sharon Miller (eds.). 1999. *Financing American Religion*. Walnut Creek, CA: AltaMira Press.

CNN. 2015. "European migrant crisis: Austria, Germany near tipping point: Pope implores European Catholics to help." September 6. http://www.cnn.com/2015/09/06/europe/europe-migrant-crisis.

Collins, Thomas Cardinal. 2013. *Cornerstones of Faith*. Toronto: Novalis.

Daly, George Thomas. 1921. *Catholic Problems in Western Canada*. Toronto: Macmillan.

Davie, Grace. 1994. *Religion in Britain Since 1945*. Oxford: Blackwell.

D'Antonio, William V., Michele Dillon, and Mary L. Gautier. 2013. *American Catholics in Transition*. Lanham, MD: Rowman & Littlefield.

De Souza, Raymond J. 2015. "A tribute to two cultures – and their twin spiritualities." *National Post*, August 3. http://news.nationalpost.com/full-comment/father-raymond-j-de-souza-a-tribute-to-two-cultures-and-their-twin-spiritualities.

———. 2015. "Losing our religion." *National Post*, September 28. http://news.nationalpost.com/full-comment/father-raymond-j-de-souza-losing-our-religion.

Dobbelaere, Karel. 2002. *Secularization: An Analysis at Three Levels*. Oxford: Oxford University Press.

Durkheim, Emile. 1965. *The Elementary Forms of the Religious Life*. New York: The Free Press. Originally published in 1912.

Engelmann, Frederick C. and Mildred A. Schwartz. 1975. *Canadian Political Parties: Origin, Character, Impact*. Toronto: Prentice-Hall.

Epatko, Larisa. 2015. "Full text of Pope Francis' remarks to Congress." PBS Newshour, September 24. http://www.pbs.org/newshour/rundown/full-text-of-pope-francis-remarks-to-congress.

Falardeau, Jean-Charles. 1976. "The Seventeenth-Century Parish in French Canada." In Stewart Crysdale and Les Wheatcroft (eds.). *Religion in Canadian Society*. Toronto: Macmillan. Pp. 101–112.

Fay, Terence. 2002. *A History of Canadian Catholics.* Montreal: McGill-Queen's University Press.

Fay, Terence J. 2009. *New Faces of Canadian Catholics: The Asians.* Toronto: Novalis.

Ferreira, Carlos. "A world without Catholic Charities?" 2013. Salt and Light TV blog, April 12.

Fergusson, Maggie. 2014. "Jean of Ark." A feature article on Jean Vanier. *Intelligent Life, The Economist.* July/August.

Flegel, Frank. 2015. "Regina launches archdiocesan appeal." *Prairie Messenger*, September 30. http://www.prairiemessenger.ca/15_09_30/dnews_15_09_30_4.html.

Freud, Sigmund. 1957. *The Future of an Illusion.* Garden City, NY: Doubleday.

Friesen, Joe. 2015. "Toronto's Catholic Archdiocese aiming to raise $3-million for refugees." September 8. *Globe and Mail*, September 8. http://www.theglobeandmail.com/news/national/torontos-catholic-archdiocese-aiming-to-raise-3-million-for-refugees/article26266781.

Froehle, Bryan T. and Mary L. Gautier. 2002. *Portrait of a World Church.* Maryknoll, NY: Orbis Books.

Garnsworthy, Lewis S. 1986. "Diocesan gathering to reflect on AngliTrends findings with Reginald Bibby." May. Toronto: Anglican Diocese.

Glatz, Carol. 2015. "Vatican welcomes its first family of refugees following pope's appeal." Catholic News Service. September 18. http://www.catholicnews.com/services/englishnews/2015/vatican-welcomes-first-refugee-family-after-papal-appeal.cfm.

Glock, Charles Y. and Rodney Stark. 1965. *Religion and Society in Tension.* Chicago: Rand McNally.

Gonzales, Ramon. 2015. "Even as a child, priest heard God's call." Story of priest from India. *Western Catholic Reporter*, September 28. http://www.wcr.ab.ca/ThisWeek/Stories/tabid/61/entryid/6907/Default.aspx.

Graham, Ron. 1990. *God's Dominion.* Toronto: McClelland and Stewart.

Grant, John Webster. 1998. *The Church in the Canadian Era.* Expanded edition. Vancouver: Regent College Publishing.

Greeley, Andrew M. 1994. "Why do Catholics stay in the Church: Because of the stories." *New York Times*, July 10. http://www.nytimes.com/1994/07/10/magazine/why-do-catholics-stay-in-the-church-because-of-the-stories.html?pagewanted=all.

———. 2010. *Chicago Catholics and the Struggle within Their Church.* New York: Transaction Publishers.

Groome, Thomas H. 2003. *What Makes Us Catholic.* San Francisco: Harper.

Gyapong, Deborah. 2011. "Novalis celebrates 75 years of bringing the liturgy to Canadians." Canadian Catholic News. Appeared in *Western Catholic Reporter*, July 18. http://www.wcr.ab.ca/ThisWeek/Stories/tabid/61/entryid/1205/Default.aspx.

———. 2015. "Ottawa Catholics gather to hear how they can help refugees." Canadian Catholic News. Appeared in *B.C. Catholic*, October 3. http://www.bccatholic.ca/canadian/5571-ottawa-catholics-gather-to-hear-how-they-can-help-refugees.

Hale, Christopher J. 2015. "The Pope Francis statement that changed the Church on LGBT issues." *Time*, July 28. http://time.com/3975630/pope-francis-lgbt-issues.

Harris, Sam. 2006. *Letter to a Christian Nation*. New York: Knopf. Vintage Book edition 2008.

Higgins, Michael W. and Douglas R. Letson. 2002. *Power and Peril: The Catholic Church at the Crossroads*. Toronto: Harper Collins.

Higgins, Michael W. and Peter Kavanagh. 2010. *Suffer the Children unto Me: An Open Inquiry into the Clerical Sex Abuse Scandal*. Toronto: Novalis.

Higgins, Michael W. and Kevin Burns. 2012. *Genius Born of Anguish: The Life & Legacy of Henri Nouwen*. New York: Paulist Press.

Higgins, Michael W. 2015. "Pope Francis's Act One in the U.S. – An invitation, not reproach." *Globe and Mail*, September 28. http://www.theglobeandmail.com/globe-debate/pope-franciss-act-one-in-the-us-an-invitation-not-reproach/article26561062.

Huel, Raymond. 1983. "The French Catholic Experience in Western Canada." In Benjamin G. Sillie (ed.). *Visions of the New Jerusalem*. Edmonton: NeWest Press. Pp. 39–53.

Hustak, Alan. 2015. "'Catholic' is removed from Montreal social agency's name." *The Catholic Register*, January 15. http://www.catholicregister.org/item/19530-catholic-is-removed-from-montreal-social-agency-s-name.

Irvine, William P. 1974. "Explaining the religious bias of the Canadian partisan identity: Success on the third try." *Canadian Journal of Political Science* 3:560–563.

Janda, Kenneth. 1980. *Political Parties: A Cross-National Survey*. New York: The Free Press.

Jensen, Kurt. 2015. "People with disabilities 'welcomed, valued' during Pope Francis' visit." Catholic News Service, October 2. http://www.catholicnews.com/services/englishnews/2015/people-with-disabilities-welcomed-valued-during-pope-francis-visit.cfm.

Jensen, Trevor and Margaret Ramirez. 2013. "Andrew Greeley dead: Priest, author, critic was 85." *Chicago Tribune*, May 30. http://www.chicagotribune.com/news/local/breaking/chi-andrew-greeley-dead-20130530-story.html.

Karimi, Faith. 2013. "Pope Francis' embrace of a severely disfigured man touches world." CNN, November 7. http://www.cnn.com/2013/11/07/world/europe/pope-francis-embrace.

Kozlowska, Hanna. 2015. "The pope warns churches to take in refugees – or else." *Quartz*, September 16. http://qz.com/503227/the-pope-warns-churches-to-take-in-refugees-or-else.

Krawczynski, Agnieszka. 2015. "New arrivals give major boost to church attendance in Toronto." *B.C. Catholic*, May 17. http://www.bccatholic.ca/canadian/5131-new-arrivals-give-major-boost-to-church-attendance-in-toronto.

Lefebvre, Solange. 2008. "The Francophone Roman Catholic Church." In Paul Bramadat and David Seljak (eds.). *Christianity and Ethnicity in Canada*. Toronto: University of Toronto Press. Pp. 49–100.

Lenski, Gerhard. 1963. *The Religious Factor*. New York: Doubleday.

Lewis, David L. 1993. "Canada's Native Peoples and the Churches." In W.E. Hewitt (ed.). *The Sociology of Religion: A Canadian Focus*. Pp. 235–252.

Longhurst, John. 2012. "'We have a deep faith in God': Filipinos help fill Catholic churches in Winnipeg." *Winnipeg Free Press*, March 3. http://www.winnipegfreepress.com/arts-and-life/life/faith/we-have-a-deep-faith-in-god-141281773.html.

McBrien, Richard P. 1992. *Report on the Church: Catholicism after Vatican II*. New York: Harper Collins.

McDonald, Lynn. 1969. "Religion and voting: A study of the 1968 Canadian federal election in Ontario." *Canadian Review of Sociology and Anthropology* 6:129–144.

McGowan, Mark. 2008. "Roman Catholics (Anglophone and Allophone)." In Paul Bramadat and David Seljak (eds.). *Christianity and Ethnicity in Canada*. Toronto: University of Toronto Press. Pp. 49–100.

Manseau, Peter. 2014. "What it means to be Catholic now." *New York Times*, March 9. http://www.nytimes.com/2014/03/10/opinion/what-it-means-to-be-catholic-now.html?_r=1.

Markoe, Lauren. 2015. "At 9/11 site, pope prays with Muslims, Jews, Sikhs, Buddhists and Hindus." Religion News Service, September 25. http://www.religionnews.com/2015/09/25/at-911-site-pope-prays-with-muslims-jews-sikhs-buddhists-and-hindus.

Marty, Martin E. 2014. "Who is a Catholic?" *Sightings*, March 17. http://divinity.uchicago.edu/sightings/who-catholic-%E2%80%94-martin-e-marty.

———. 2015. "Annulments and change." *Sightings*, September 14. http://divinity.uchicago.edu/sightings/annulments-and-change.

Mead, Walter Russell. 2010. "Pentecostal power." A blog in *The American Interest*. May 28.

Miller, Archbishop J. Michael. 2006. *The Holy See's Teaching on Catholic Schools*. Manchester, NH: Sophia Institute Press.

———. 2015. "Parents as Primary Evangelists and Catechists." Presented at the World Meeting of Families in Philadelphia, September 23. *BC Catholic*, October 2. http://www.bccatholic.ca/opinion-and-editorial/5583-parents-as-primary-evangelists-and-catechists.

Mol, Hans. 1985. *Faith and Fragility: Religion and Identity in Canada*. Burlington: Trinity Press.

Moreux, Colette. 1976. "The End of a Religion?" In Stewart Crysdale and Les Wheatcroft (eds.). *Religion in Canadian Society*. Toronto: Macmillan. Pp. 359–371.

Murphy, Terrence and Roberto Perin (eds.). 1996. *A Concise History of Christianity in Canada*. Toronto: Oxford.

Noll, Mark A. and Carolyn Nystrom. 2005. *Is the Reformation Over? An Evangelical Assessment of Contemporary Roman Catholicism*. Grand Rapids, MI: Baker Academic.

Noll, Mark A. 1992. *A History of Christianity in the United States and Canada*. Grand Rapids, MI: William B. Eerdmans.

———. 2007. *What Happened to Christian Canada?* Vancouver: Regent College Publishing.

Nouwen, Henri J.M. 1998. *Sabbatical Journey: The Diary of His Final Year*. New York: Crossroad Publishing.

———. 2011. *A Spirituality of Living*. Nashville: Upper Room Books.

Peck, M. Scott. 1978. *The Road Less Traveled*. New York: Random House.

Peritz, Ingrid. 2010. "As churches crumble, communities fear loss of heritage." *Globe and Mail*. December 14. http://www.theglobeandmail.com/news/national/as-churches-crumble-communities-fear-loss-of-heritage/article1320111.

Persichilli, Angelo. 2010. "Resilient church will overcome latest scandal." *Toronto Star*. April 4. http://www.thestar.com/news/world/2010/04/04/persichilli_resilient_church_will_overcome_latest_scandal.html.

Pew Research Center. 2006. "Spirit and power: A 10-country survey of Pentecostals." October 5. http://www.pewforum.org/2006/10/05/spirit-and-power.

———. 2013. *The Global Catholic Population*. February 12, 2013. http://www.pewglobal.org/2014search/?query=global catholic population.

———. 2014. *Origins and Destinations of the World's Migrants, from 1990-2013*. September 2. http://www.pewforum.org/2013/02/13/the-global-catholic-population.

———. 2015. *The Future of World Religions: Population Growth Projections, 2010-2050*. April 2. http://www.pewforum.org/2015/04/02/religious-projections-2010-2050.

Phan, Rachel. 2012. "Tithing in Canada: Churchgoers divided over donating percentage of their income." *Huffington Post Canada*, August 12. http://www.huffingtonpost.ca/ 2012/08/12/tithing-canada-church_n_1703526.html.

Regenstreif, S. Peter. 1964. "Group Perceptions and the Vote." In John Meisel (ed.). *Papers on the 1962 Election*. Toronto: University of Toronto Press.

Regnier, André. 2012. *Catholic Missionary Identity*. Ottawa: Catholic Christian Outreach.

Reid, Angus. 1996. *Shakedown: How the New Economy Is Changing Our* Lives. Toronto: Doubleday.

Reynolds, Neil. 2011. "The globalization of God in the 21st century." *Globe and Mail*. January 10. http://www.theglobeandmail.com/globe-debate/the-globalization-of-god-in-the-21st-century/article621583.

Rioux, Marcel. 1978. *Quebec in Question*. James Boake (trans.). Toronto: James Lorimer.

Rokeach, Milton. 1973. *The Nature of Human Values*. New York: Free Press.

Rolheiser, Ronald. 2006. *Secularity and the Gospel: Being Missionaries to Our Children*. New York: Crossroad.

———. 2014. *The Holy Longing: The Search for a Christian Spirituality*. New York: Random House.

———. 2015. "Principles for interfaith dialogue and interfaith attitudes." April 13. Column archives. Ron Rolheiser, OMI. http://ronrolheiser.com/principles-for-interfaith-dialogue-and-interfaith-attitudes/#.VfyXShFRGUk.

Roof, Wade Clark. 1999. *Spiritual Marketplace: Baby Boomers and the Remaking of American Religion*. Princeton, NJ: Princeton University Press.

Rouleau, Jean-Paul. 1977. "Religion in Quebec: Present and Future." *Pro Mundi Vita: Dossiers*. Nov–Dec, No. 3.

Saad, Lydia. 2009. "Churchgoing among U.S. Catholics slides to tie Protestants." Washington, DC: Gallup Poll. April 9.

———. 2012. "U.S. confidence in organized religion at low point." Washington, DC: Gallup Poll. July 12.

———. 2015. "Confidence in religion at new low, but not among Catholics." Washington, DC: Gallup Poll. June 17.

Seljak, David. 1995. "Why the Quiet Revolution was 'quiet': The Catholic Church's reaction to the secularization of nationalism in Quebec after 1960." *Historical Studies* 62:109–124.

———. 2000. "Resisting the 'No Man's Land' of Private Religion." In David Lyon and Marguerite Van Die (eds.). *Rethinking Church, State and Modernity*. Toronto: University of Toronto Press. Pp. 131–148.

Sévigny, Robert. 1976. "The Religious Experience of Youth in Quebec." In Stewart Crysdale and Les Wheatcroft (eds.). *Religion in Canadian Society*. Toronto: Macmillan. Pp. 485–496.

Shimpo, Mitsuru. 1976. "Native Religion in Sociocultural Change: The Cree and Saulteaux in Southern Saskatchewan, 1830–1900." In Stewart Crysdale and Les Wheatcroft (eds.). *Religion in Canadian Society*. Toronto: Macmillan. Pp. 128–140.

Sinasac, Joseph. 2015. "Yes, there is a Catholic journalism." *Western Catholic Reporter*, September 28. http://www.wcr.ab.ca/ThisWeek/Stories/tabid/61/entryid/6899/Default.aspx.

Smith, Christian, Jonathan Hill, and Kari Christoffersen. 2014. *Young Catholic America: Emerging Adults In, Out of, and Gone from the Church*. New York: Oxford University Press.

Smith, Tom W. 2009. *Religious Change around the World*. Report prepared for the Templeton Foundation. http://news.uchicago.edu/files/religionsurvey_20091023.pdf.

Stark, Rodney, 2015. *The Triumph of Faith*. Wilmington, DE: ISI Books.

——— and Charles Y. Glock. 1968. *American Piety*. Berkeley: University of California Press.

Statistics Canada, Demography Division. 2012a. "Table 1.4. Annual number of immigrants observed (2008/2009) and projected (2035/2036) according to three assumptions, Canada, provinces, and territories." Cat. No. 91-520-X. http://www.statcan.gc.ca/pub/91-520-x/2010001/t470-eng.htm.

Statistics Canada. 2012b. "Population growth in Canada: From 1851 to 2061." Cat. 98-310-X-2011003. Modified. 2013-12-18.

Sutherland, Anne. 2010. "Quebecers celebrate St. Brother Andre." *The National Post*. Holy Post. October 30. http://news.nationalpost.com/holy-post/quebecers-celebrate-st-brother-andre.

Swan, Michael. 2015. "New York goes crazy in a papal sort of way." *The Catholic Register*, September 25. http://www.catholicregister.org/francisintheusa/item/20953-new-york-goes-crazy-in-a-papal-sort-of-way.

Tablet, The. 2015. "No one separated from love of God." Editorial. September 3. http://www.thetablet.co.uk/editors-desk/1/6591/no-one-separated-from-love-of-god.

Taylor, Charles. 1989. *Sources of the Self.* Cambridge, MA: Harvard University Press.

———. 2007. *A Secular Age*. Cambridge, MA: Harvard University Press.

Thanh Ha, Tu. 2010. "Vatican, Canadian church officials tried to keep sex scandal secret." *Globe and Mail*, April 9. http://www.theglobeandmail.com/news/national/vatican-canadian-church-officials-tried-to-keep-sex-scandal-secret/article4315371.

Tickle, Phyllis. 2008. *The Great Emergence: How Christianity is Changing and Why*. Ada, MI: Baker Books.

Thomson, Janet and Manmeet Ahluwalia. 2013. "Catholic church findings followers in ethnic communities." March 13. http://www.cbc.ca/news/canada/catholic-church-finding-followers-in-ethnic-communities-1.1310449.

Todd, Douglas. 2010. "Five spiritual trends for the '10s." *Vancouver Sun*. January 9. http://blogs.vancouversun.com/2010/01/09/five-spiritual-trends-for-the-10s.

Turcotte, Martin. 2012. *Charitable Giving by Canadians*. Ottawa: Statistics Canada, Cat. No. 11-008-X. April 16. http://www.statcan.gc.ca/pub/11-008-x/2012001/article/11637-eng.pdf.

Twain, Mark. 1881. "Mark Twain in Montreal: His speech at the banquet in his honor." *New York Times*, December 10, 1881. http://www.twainquotes.com/18811210.html.

U.S. News and World Report. 2015. "Pope kisses forehead of disabled boy after landing at Philadelphia airport." AP. September 26. http://www.usnews.com/news/us/articles/2015/09/26/at-philadelphia-airport-pope-kisses-head-of-disabled-boy.

Valpy, Michael and Joe Friesen. 2010. "Canada marching from religion to secularization." *Globe and Mail*. December 10. http://www.theglobeandmail.com/news/national/canada-marching-from-religion-to-secularization/article1320108.

Vanier, Jean. 2010. *Becoming Human*. CBC Massey Lectures, 1998. Third edition. Toronto: Anansi.

———. 2015. *Signs: Seven Words of Hope*. Toronto: Novalis.

Wente, Margaret. 2015. "Why does everybody have a Popecrush?" *Globe and Mail*, September 22. http://www.theglobeandmail.com/globe-debate/why-does-everybody-have-a-popecrush/article26464579.

Westhues, Kenneth. 1976. "The Adaptation of the Roman Catholic Church in Canadian Society." In Stewart Crysdale and Les Wheatcroft (eds.). *Religion in Canadian Society*. Toronto: Macmillan. Pp. 290–306.

Wilkins-Laflamme, Sarah. 2016. "Protestant and Catholic distinctions in secularization." *Journal of Contemporary Religion*. In press.

Wilson, Bryan. 1966. *Religion in Secular Society*. London: CA Watts.

Winfield, Nicole and Andrea Rodriguez. 2015. "Pope urges Cuba to 'be willing to change.'" AP in *Time*, September 21.

Wooden, Cindy. 2015. "Pope tells priests to offer forgiveness for abortion." Catholic News Service, September 2.

Yakabuski, Konrad. 2009. "Neither practising nor believing, but Catholic even so." *Globe and Mail*, August 14. http://www.theglobeandmail.com/globe-debate/neither-practising-nor-believing-but-catholic-even-so/article4329828/?page=all.

Yardley, Jim. 2015. "A humble pope, challenging the world." *New York Times*, September 18. http://www.nytimes.com/2015/09/19/world/europe/pope-francis.html?_r=0.

Yinger, J. Milton. 1971. *The Scientific Study of Religion*. New York: Macmillan.

Index